Teleselling Techniques That Close the Sale

Teleselling Techniques That Close the Sale

Flyn L. Penoyer

AMACOM
American Management Association

New York • Atlanta • Boston • Chicago • Kansas City • San Francisco • Washington, D.C.
Brussels • Mexico City • Tokyo • Toronto

*This publication is designed to provide accurate and authoritative in-
formation in regard to the subject matter covered. It is sold with the
understanding that the publisher is not engaged in rendering legal,
accounting, or other professional service. If legal advice or other expert
assistance is required, the services of a competent professional person
should be sought.*

Library of Congress Cataloging-in-Publication Data

Penoyer, Flyn L.
    Teleselling techniques that close the sale / Flyn L. Penoyer.
        p. cm.
    Includes index.
    ISBN 0-8144-7939-1
    1. Telephone selling. I. Title.
HF5438.3.P46 1997
658.8'4—dc21   97–5372
                                                                      CIP

Printing number

10 9 8 7 6 5 4 3 2 1

CONTENTS

Contents

WHO SHOULD READ THIS BOOK?

Teleselling Techniques That Close the Sale was specifically written for the telesales professional looking to improve his or her telephone sales skills. The book will also be invaluable to sales managers who wish to brush up their skills or are looking for training material for use with their people. If you are a sales professional who depends on the telephone for your livelihood, you will find this work a valuable tool in perfecting your telephone sales presentation. In addition, you may find many of the techniques presented in the following chapters valuable in face-to-face selling.

This book does not teach you how to sell, either on the phone or in person. That is not its purpose. It deals directly with the ingredients that make up a good telephone call. During the course of the book, I cover eight subjects that, when combined in your telephone selling effort, will give you the maximum chance for success. My purpose is to define those critical tasks or functions that must be part of a telephone sales call if it is to be successful.

The goal is to give you both the knowledge and the ability to implement the methods and techniques presented. At the end of each chapter you will find tips on how you can work on your own skills and some self-training instructional exercises that will assist you in implementing the material presented. I will also present you with a self-training method, tape training, that you can use to perfect your techniques. It is a method of self-evaluation that will help you master the methods in this book and all phases of your sales call.

Your success requires only your consistent effort. Remember that learning how to do something well takes not only effort but patience. You may find that your current telephone habits are hard to break. At first you may even find that you are not sure what the deficiency in your presentation is. In addition, you may not completely understand just how to implement these principles, and it may take multiple attempts before you master some of the concepts and techniques described. As I said, be patient. Your only hope of success is repeated effort and experimentation with these new methods.

I can only assure you that if you practice the concepts in this book, you will see a transformation in your ability to succeed on the telephone. You don't need to be a super salesperson or have a sales trainer to be successful. This book and some basic elbow grease will make you better on the telephone.

INTRODUCTION

Hello, and welcome to *Teleselling Techniques That Close the Sale*. It has been my goal for years to put on paper the knowledge of telephone selling that I have gained. I have reviewed many sales materials, including a large number of telemarketing books, and I have been disappointed by their inability or lack of effort to really teach the reader how to make better calls. This book is written from my personal experience and knowledge of telemarketing and telesales. For the past twenty-four years my career has been focused on telesales. For the last fifteen years I have managed and implemented business-to-business telephone sales programs for the electronics and computer industry.

I started my career in the early 1970s with a magazine distributor, where I received some excellent training. I spent a total of six or so years in consumer telesales management and sales positions that focused on the telephone. In the early 1980s I began my career in the management of telesales operations for the electronics industry. Since then I have managed for a number of major companies, including Dysan (a floppy disk manufacturer), Memorex (computer communications products), and Logitech (a computer mouse manufacturer). For the last ten years I have primarily been a consultant to the computer industry in this field, providing all phases of telesales and telemarketing development. I have set up scores of organizations from scratch and trained over a thousand salespeople to sell on the telephone. It is with this experience that I hope to help you master the telephone. I use what I preach, and I believe it is the reason I can close one out of every five prospects I add to my database.

The information presented in this book is not complex, nor is it likely to be anything the experienced salesperson hasn't heard before. Sales is sales, and though the telephone has some unique properties, there is not much new to say about it. What is evidently true is that most salespeople don't employ the proper methods and techniques, even if they are familiar with them— and many don't know or understand these techniques well enough to implement them in their telephone sales efforts.

My objective in this book is teach you what works on the telephone, and then help you learn how to apply it to your own sales calls. If I can bring you to the point where you listen to your own calls constructively, looking for the proper or best way to proceed, then you will start, based on what you have been taught, to improve yourself almost automatically, using the techniques in this book.

Amazingly, once you have learned the theoretical material and start using the self-training methods recommended, you will find yourself able to correct your course even during the sales call. This comes from an acute awareness of what is transpiring during the sales call itself. You will develop this awareness by listening to your own calls with a critical ear and comparing them to the methods and techniques you learn in this book.

This book has a number of features to assist you in mastering the telephone skills presented. It offers both facts and theory that you can study and learn. To help you apply that theory, I have included some carefully constructed self-study role-plays that, when performed, will help you understand and apply the techniques discussed. You will also find actual sales calls that have been annotated and analyzed to help you better understand the methods discussed. And finally, you will find self-tests to challenge your basic knowledge of the theory and assist you in confirming your knowledge.

Well, off to our adventure . . . good luck and good selling!

ONE

WHAT YOU WILL LEARN, AND HOW TO USE THIS BOOK

It is my objective to help you to understand the real nature of telephone selling. In addition, it is my goal to get you to listen to what is taking place in your sales calls and to recognize more selling opportunities than you ever have before. I hope to impart an understanding of those things that are necessary to making a successful telephone sales call.

To be truly successful with the tools I provide, you must become so familiar with them that you begin to analyze yourself as you make your sales presentation. You will find it reasonably easy to listen to calls you have made and discover many opportunities to improve your presentation. Finding such opportunities as you make the call is a bit more difficult and requires a real mastery of the methods and techniques.

WHAT WILL YOU LEARN?

This book contains ten chapters—eight of which deal with the techniques and methods that I believe are the keys to successful telephone selling. Combined in a sales call, these eight techniques will maximize your chances for success. The eight keys to successful telephone selling are:

1. Understanding the telephone as a sales tool
2. Having the right attitude for success
3. Using your voice properly
4. Understanding the importance of decision makers
5. Proper qualifying
6. Setting and using call objectives to guide your presentation
7. Being persistently curious and investigative to find opportunities
8. Closing properly and relentlessly throughout the presentation

Each one of these techniques by itself will improve your ability to succeed on the phone; in combination, they have the ability to make you a professional of the highest caliber.

In addition to the theoretical information, you will find

hints and exercises to help you master the material. Also, some of the chapters include transcripts from actual calls (with names and other details changed to protect the actual participants) that serve as examples to help you better understand the concepts. Finally, I present you with a method for training yourself using self-evaluation. Whether or not you have someone to help you in your sales education, you will find the methods useful in significantly improving your abilities on the phone.

How to Use This Book

Because the material in the book is so interdependent, first read the book as you might a novel, skipping over the exercises, to get a complete overview of the concepts and ideas. After your first reading you will have a general knowledge of the concepts and be able to start implementing them immediately.

Once you have finished your first reading, I suggest that you go through each chapter in detail, doing the exercises and making sure you completely understand the concepts before proceeding to the next section. This second reading will help you further in your implementation, making you more precise and complete in your effort at each task. As you come back for this second reading, you will have the added advantage of knowing how things tie together.

By this time you should have a very complete understanding of the methods and techniques presented. You are now ready to start the detailed process of implementing them in your own presentation. At this point, I suggest you go through each section with the idea of creating a list of questions and tasks that need to be a part of your presentation. Then, using the tape method described later in the book, make at least three to five different tapes of your calls and extensively analyze these tapes afterwards, making corrections to your presentation and then repeating the process. Master each technique individually, attempting to use it to its fullest. Each chapter contains exercises that will help you to master the techniques.

Finally, set up a regular taping program (see Chapter 10 for instructions on how to use the tapes to improve your calls). Use the book as a reference to analyze your calls and determine the areas in which you need help. Then use the book again to re-think and fine-tune your approach. By this time you should see significant progress in your telephone skills.

TWO

THE TELEPHONE AS A SALES TOOL

The Telephone Selling Environment

One of the most important things to understand about telephone selling is the nature of the environment in which the telephone forces you to communicate. Although the telephone is a commonly used medium for communication, it is not the normal environment in which we are accustomed to exchanging ideas. We are more used to seeing the other person as we communicate, reading his or her body language and comprehending it along with the words. We have grown from childhood to depend on these many visual and environmental clues to understanding our parents and others with whom we communicate. On the telephone, most of these inputs don't exist. Thus, to communicate as effectively on the telephone as we do in person, we must find new ways of completing the communication process and filling in the missing pieces of information that in personal communication come to us from visual contact.

Before we can be successful on the telephone, we must understand the nature of our communication with our prospects or customers. Remember, this is not the normal telephone communication you might engage in with your friends or relatives. In a telephone sales call, a great many stresses and strains come into play that are not present in our everyday use of the phone. It is these differences between the personal call and the sales call that we must discover. It is our knowledge of these things that allows us to better communicate in our telephone sales effort.

What Is a Telephone Sales Presentation?

Let's start by asking, So what *is* a telephone sales call? Your first answer might include an effort to persuade, an effort to develop rapport, an effort to educate, or an attempt to close a deal. But these are really just parts of the telephone sales call, not its true nature. Take a car, for example. What is its true nature? You might say its wheels, seats, motor, and so on, but your car is not these things, it is made of and from these things. By its nature, your car is really a vehicle, a method of transportation from point to point. In the same way, your telephone sales call is really a commercial. When you think about the purpose of television and radio commercials or print advertising, you begin to see the similarity. Realizing that your telephone sales call is actually a commercial is the most important thing you can do to begin to understand what will be necessary for it to succeed. If you compare the pieces of the sales call listed above, you will discover that each of them is a part of almost all ordinary commercials.

This being true, if a telephone sales presentation really is a commercial, then we must seriously consider how we will present it (telephone sales presentation) to our prospects. Why? Because people generally react negatively to commercials. You've received telephone solicitations. What was your reaction? In a selling situation we certainly don't want to add any negatives to the presentation of our products or services. It is hard enough to make a sale without presenting negatives to our prospects, intentionally or not. In other words, we want to make sure the call is a very positive experience for our prospects because we want them to make the decision to buy!

Probably the greatest obstacle to telephone success is the salesperson's failure to understand the nature and environment of the telephone sales call. Like it or not, a telephone sales call is a commercial, and that affects the way we need to present ourselves. A clear understanding of this point forces us to change the way we deliver our presentation. You don't talk to a prospect or customer the way you would talk to a friend or relative. Many salespeople will argue that the way they talk isn't really all that important. But because your presentation is a commercial, it carries negatives just by its nature. These negatives must be accounted for and overcome if you are to be successful. As with anything in the universe, failure to deal with the true nature of the situation results in destruction. Those who take into account the nature of the telephone can master it. Those who don't simply wonder what went wrong and what happened to their sale.

Let's try to understand the nature of our commercial a little better by investigating what a commercial actually is. Let's also compare our presentation with other commercials we may be competing against for the prospect's attention. By comparing our interface with the customer with that of other commercials, what is important about our presentation will become clear. After all, if we are going to be successful in selling the prospect, we must have his or her full attention. If we are a commercial, this means we had better be a good one.

Ask yourself the following questions: "How do I react to commercials, even telephone sales calls?" "How much time do I give the seller in these situations to get my attention?" "What does the seller have to do to get my positive attention and decision to listen, and, even more important, to buy?" If you are like most of us, you find commercials something of an annoyance, probably just because of the sheer volume you are forced to consume each day. Everywhere you go you see billboards, hear advertisements, and get pitched for one product or another. Your prospects suffer the same fate; they too are bombarded with ads and calls from salespeople trying to get their business. If your prospects are decision makers (at home or in a business), all your competitors' salespeople are probably calling them as well, not to mention all the other companies trying to get a share of their business.

The point is, you have some very stiff competition for a prospect's ear. Not only must you compete with all the other salespeople and commercials in the world, but you must also compete for that person's time within his or her current environment. If at home, the prospect may be involved in a hobby, watching TV, or interacting with the family. The business person, on the other hand, may be involved in any number of projects or deadlines that are completely unknown to you. In order to get a prospect's attention, especially on the phone, you will need to be special. Being special is the only way you can hope to stand out from the barrage of information being tossed in the prospect's direction. Being special is the only way to really get the prospect's attention. Finally, being special is probably the only way you can differentiate your me-too products from the competition.

Before we talk specifically about how this is accomplished, let's take a look at your commercial competition and how it stacks up. By looking at the other commercials your prospect is receiving, you can see the strengths and weaknesses of your own presentation.

Radio vs. Telephone Commercials

Radio commercials are probably one of your biggest competitors, not necessarily for your products or services, but for your prospects' attention. Most people listen to the radio regularly. What does a radio commercial have that you don't?

1. *Sound.* Radio has music and sound effects that don't generally exist in a telephone sales call. I guess you could make a tape of sound effects, even background music, and play it as you give your presentation, but this probably isn't very practical.
2. *Multiple voices.* Radio also very often uses multiple voices to tell its story.
3. *Professional voices.* As we all know, there are few commercials in which you don't hear extremely pleasing voices. I know they are better than mine, at least.
4. *Professional scripts.* Of course, everything you hear on radio is scripted. Carefully thought out descriptions, jokes, and closes make up what you hear. There is no stuttering, hesitation, or pauses of confusion, just a nice clean perfect presentation of the material.

If we consider television, we add video to the tools and advantages these external commercials have.

Imagine how you sound compared to these commercials. Are you as interesting, as funny, as pleasing to listen to as a professional voice? If you, as a consumer of commercials, turn off these presentations, with all their splendor, how do you think you would react to your own presentation? Would you turn it off? These are key questions in understanding the quality of your telephone sales message.

Next we'll look at the face-to-face selling situation and see what can be learned about our sales call.

Face-to-Face Selling vs. Telephone Selling

Let's examine the differences between your telephone sales presentation and a face-to-face effort. This will provide some additional input that is useful in constructing a powerful telephone presentation.

The differences between the telephone and face-to-face are:

1. *Control.* In a face-to-face situation you have more control than you have on the phone. Being there in person gives you a bit more control over the situation. It is possible to be thrown out of someone's office; however, it is far easier for the prospect to make an excuse and hang up the phone than to end a meeting. It is important to remember that there is a time limit on every call, and if you're not in control, it may show up at a not-so-convenient time.

2. *Mutual vision.* There are a number of key factors that come into play because of your ability to see the prospect and his or her ability to see you. The first is the ability to see the prospect's environment. When on the phone, one does not see the prospect's business environment. The environment may contain clues as to the size of the company, products in use, or additional items that might be needed. Second, and one of the most important factors, your ability to determine the prospect's attentiveness to your presentation is severely limited by your lack of vision. In addition, when you are there in person, you receive visual clues to the prospect's feelings about your presentation.

3. *Demonstration.* This is, of course, a product of vision as well, but it is also a feature of selling that completely changes on the phone. It's not just the fact that you can't demonstrate the physical products, but the fact that any attempt to display a solution or answer becomes more complicated.

What's Most Important?

Now that we have investigated the realm of the commercial, you can see there are a number of key factors in your presentation that are affected. There are things to take into account that you might miss if you aren't specifically aware of the differences. Think for a minute about how these different aspects of the commercial affect what you do, then ask yourself the following questions.

1. Where does your customer get his or her picture of you?
2. Where does your customer get his or her picture of your product?
3. Where does your customer get his or her picture of your company?
4. Where does your customer get his or her excitement for your product?
5. Where does all the *sizzle* of your presentation come from?

In a face-to-face encounter, the prospect sees these things with his or her eyes; in your telephone presentation, they all come from one thing: your voice! You must always remember that your voice is the most important piece of your presentation. It's not that you must have a spectacular voice, but that your voice is the medium that transmits all the critical information to your customers and prospects. It is, as they say, the *sizzle* that will sell the steak! All the competitive commercials, including other salespeople and the prospect's or customer's environment, force you to compete for attention with the quality of your presentation. The only tool you have to transmit this information is your voice.

EVERY TELEPHONE CALL HAS A TIME LIMIT!

Time is limited in a telephone call. When you meet with a prospect, an hour or even two is not a long time to stay at his or her office. People associate meetings with hours. The telephone, on the other hand, is quite different. Telephone calls seem long after ten or fifteen minutes. Because you don't have control of the situation, as you would if you were sitting in the prospect's office, you have an unseen time limit.

Because the prospect can easily end a telephone conversation, you are at risk throughout your presentation of running out of time. If the prospect gets tired, irritated, bored, or whatever, that might be the excuse to cut short your presentation. The nature of the telephone means you must be interesting, efficient, and always moving forward through your sales presentation or you may be cut off.

THE COMPETITION IS FIERCE!

You may still be asking yourself: Why is it so important to be special? The main reason is that you must differentiate yourself from all the competition, and on the telephone you must get the person's attention.

As you know from getting sales calls yourself, the first challenge is to get the prospect's attention. Most people have a large resistance to a stranger calling them on the phone. We put up an immediate defense screen. For the businessperson, this screen may be even more substantial because time is the businessman's enemy; he never has enough. Even more important may be the fact that you're not the only one calling! If you have the decision maker on the phone, this means he or she makes these decisions for any number of areas—every telephone salesperson in your business is trying to reach this person, not to mention all the other people who have questions about products and services that require this person's approval.

Under these circumstances, how can you expect to be average and get the attention you need? You have to find a way to make yourself different from everyone else; otherwise you are completely dependent on the luck of the draw.

INTER-ACTIVITY: OUR BIGGEST ADVANTAGE

Our biggest advantage on the telephone is the existence of our ability to interact with the prospect. Where a television or radio commercial just tells the story blindly, we can interact with the prospect determining and focusing his or her interests. We can answer questions and deal with the specific needs of the customer as they come up. If, when listening to a radio or television commercial, the prospect has a problem, he may just disconnect, change the frequency or channel, or turn off the set. We, in our interactive environment, are able to respond to these issues directly.

Although inter-activity is a giant advantage, when you look at the commercial comparison chart (Figure 1), you see that we have many more disadvantages. The telephone sales presenta-

Figure 1. Commercial comparison.

Telephone Sales Presentation	Radio Commercial	TV Commercial	Face-to-Face Sale
Has: *Interactive Voice*	Has: *Music* *Multiple Voices* *Sound Effects* *Professional Scripts* *Story-Telling*	Has: *Music* *Multiple Voices* *Sound Effects* *Professional Scripts* *Story-Telling* *Video* *Ability to Demo*	Has: *Interactive Voice* *Visual Feedback* *Visual Clues* *Ability to Live Demo* *Control by Presence*
Doesn't Have: *Vision* *Sound, Music, or Effects* *Control* *Story-Telling* *Ability to Demo*	Doesn't Have: *Interactivity* *Video* *Control* *Ability to Demo*	Doesn't Have: *Interactivity* *Control*	Doesn't Have: *Sound, Music, or Effects*

tion exists in the most limited environment of all the commercials. It is necessary, if we wish to be successful in this limited space, that you use the inter-activity to make up for the other weaknesses that exist in your presentation.

Inter-activity has to become your eyes. All the visual clues about the prospect, his or her understanding, and feelings have to be received through this inter-activity. You must listen for the prospect's feelings and impressions. Additionally, you must ask questions to see all the clues of the environment and competitive products. Without this vision you will be lost as to the needs and desires of the prospect; you will never be able to determine what is really important.

What Have We Learned?

- The telephone sales presentation is a commercial.
- Selling on the telephone is different from face-to-face selling in many important ways.
- Understanding the true nature of our selling environment will help us to master it and make better presentations.
- Our prospects have many demands for their attention, and thus we must be special if we wish to succeed.
- Getting a prospect's attention requires real effort.
- Our voice is the essence of our telephone sales effort.
- The telephone sales presentation has an unseen time limit.

The First Rule of Telephone Selling

- Your voice is everything in a telephone sales presentation.

Chapter 2 Challenge

Refer back to the five questions posed in the section "What's Most Important?" and list some ideas you have for answers to them and what these answers might mean for your call.

See if you can figure out what is your biggest advantage over media-type commercials. List some of the key implications of this advantage.

Practice

1. Think about your product or service and come up with good reasons why you can be excited about what you sell. Your product doesn't have to be the best in the world, it just has to have value. Learn what the values of your product are and use them as your tools to be excited about what you sell.
2. Do the above for your company.
3. During each call, think about how you sound. Use your recorder to examine your calls for that positive, enthusiastic-sounding presentation.
4. Keep in mind at all times that this is a commercial, and you want your prospect to enjoy it.

Coming Up

In Chapter 4 I discuss your voice in great detail. You will learn how to make your presentation sparkle. In Chapter 3, I talk about your attitude, which is a primary factor in the success of all endeavors, especially telephone selling.

THREE

ENERGY, ENTHUSIASM, AND PASSION

Energy, enthusiasm, and *passion* are the keys to successful telephone presenting. I call them the *three jewels of the telephone.* Because we naturally transmit our feelings over the telephone, it is extremely beneficial to have these three jewels as a part of our nature, or at least as a part of our sales presentation. Without them, you are hopelessly lost in your effort to be really successful on the telephone.

Think about how you feel when you are buying something. Either you have a real need and are comfortable with the buying environment (the salesperson and the company you are purchasing from), or you are excited about the purchase you are about to make (such as a car). Can you remember a situation in which you weren't comfortable or excited but you still made the purchase? It's much rarer, right? Usually, when you don't feel good about the situation, you don't take any action. So as a salesperson, if you can get the prospect excited, you have significantly increased your chance of making the sale. The three jewels, energy, enthusiasm, and passion, are the keys to making this happen.

PERFECT TRANSMISSION

The telephone is a perfect transmitter of emotions and feelings. For some reason, even though it sometimes takes five tries to understand someone's name, feelings get transmitted in an instant; almost as soon as you open your mouth, a complete emotional package is sent to the person on the other end of the phone.

Your feelings are absolutely contagious. When you walk down the street, you react to people, and they react to you in kind. This is true not only in person, but on the telephone. Because you don't have all the visual aids to transmitting your feelings (such as a smile, a handshake, etc.), your emotions are limited completely to your voice. This causes the prospect to be more focused on how you sound, from which he or she makes judgments about who you are, and makes them instantly. It is important to remember that whatever it is you've got, your prospect is probably going to catch. If you're boring, your prospect will be bored; if you're smiling, your prospect will smile with you; and if you get excited, your prospect will follow. This is probably the reason that David Ogilvy wrote in his book *Confessions of an Advertising Man*,

> You cannot bore people into buying your product, you can only interest them in it.

Although he was probably speaking of media copy, it can certainly be assumed that a salesperson who is not very excited about his or her products, and thus gives a lackluster presentation, is going to have considerable trouble getting the prospect excited about those same products.

THE TELEPHONE: POOR TRANSMITTER OF DATA

Unfortunately, the telephone is not such a good transmitter of data. You have probably had the experience of trying to understand someone's name, maybe trying to get the correct spelling, and you just can't make it out. This is the perfect example of our dependence on visual clues to hear and understand others in a conversation. It is also the reason you must be more dynamic when selling on the phone.

Many people in their discomfort of talking to someone with whom they have no relationship are hesitant to say they can't hear or didn't understand what you said. If that information happens to be critical to your presentation, you will later get objections and questions that will interrupt the flow of your sales effort.

You will find that when you're really energized, people can hear you and do understand better what you say—not to mention they find it contagious to be around a positive individual. Remember: You must project on the phone to make up for the lack of vision in communication.

A CLOSE IN EVERY CALL

Remember, someone gets closed in every sales call! Either the salesperson closes the prospect on his or her wares, or the prospect closes the salesperson on putting off the buying decision for now. You can't always expect the prospect to follow you blindly; sometimes you have to carry her or him. It is these three jewels that will allow you to succeed in this task.

Just to make sure you understand what these jewels are, let me define each briefly as they apply to a telephone sales presentation.

Energy

Everything starts with energy, and energy is definitely the primary jewel of the three. If you have true energy for what you do, you will rarely have a problem with enthusiasm and passion, as they are natural byproducts of energy. In the twenty or so years I have been involved in the management of salespeople, I have never met an energetic salesperson who didn't carry a certain amount of enthusiasm and passion. Your success on the telephone is dependent on your possessing this trait.

Making buying decisions is tough work. It takes energy. You have to be motivated in some way to make a buying decision, or you will surely procrastinate. If you think about it, you will realize that the motivation to make any decision comes from, or even possibly is, energy. The energy to improve yourself gives you the motivation to make the decision to get a better job.

Your prospects, like you, need energy to make these decisions. The question is, where will they get that energy? To our surprise, they sometimes have it before we call. In fact, some prospects have so much energy to buy that no matter how badly we make our presentation, and in spite of everything we do to stop them, they still place their order for our product or service. But what do we do when the prospect doesn't have the energy to make the buying decision? How can we give the prospect the boost he or she needs?

The answer lies in the earlier statement that your prospect will probably catch whatever it is you have. If you are energetic about your products, you are likely to transmit some of those feelings to your prospect. Combined with the other jewels of the telephone, enthusiasm and passion, you can carry the prospect toward your goal, and eventually make the sale.

There is a byproduct of energy that most people never realize. It is only when you have become a real professional that you finally realize how rarely you have a tough call, how much trouble you have finding anyone who isn't interested in what you do or have to offer. When you talk to others, you are often surprised to find out how many negative prospects they talk to each day, and how few of their prospects are interested in what they have to offer. You start to wonder if you just got lucky and called the right people, and then it occurs to you that you're calling the same folks they are, but you're carrying them by transmitting energy.

I recently made this discovery in my consulting business, after trying to have others prospect for me. To my astonishment, they seemed lucky to find one in ten individuals who were even interested in our information, when, at the same time, I was closing revenue in almost 25 percent of my own prospects, and almost everyone seemed interested. I attribute these results to the fact that I have fun in almost every call, which in turn means that my prospects are having fun as well. If the prospects are having fun, they are much more willing to listen and discuss the opportunities I have to offer—thus a higher rate of closes and fewer difficult calls.

Enthusiasm and Passion

> What is enthusiasm? According to Webster, the definition is: *1 a:* belief in special revelations of the Holy Spirit *b:* religious fanatacism *2 a:* strong excitement of feeling: ARDOR *b:* something inspiring zeal or fervor *syn* see PASSION

Note the references to religion. Have you ever watched the evangelists? Are they enthusiastic? Are they passionate? You bet they are! What kind of results do they achieve? Do they attract people and money in large quantities? All the time! Do you see in this definition words that describe you? Look again.

21

1 a: *belief* in special revelations of the Holy Spirit b: religious *fanaticism* 2 a: strong *excitement* of feeling: *ARDOR* b: something inspiring *zeal* or *fervor* syn see *PASSION*

If you don't see words that describe yourself as you sell on the telephone, then you probably don't sell with enough *enthusiasm!*

Now let's look at some reasons why you might be so enthusiastic, so passionate, about your job. Consider the potential value your product or service has to the prospect. Think about that value and how much benefit there really is to owning the product or service you sell. Every business provides some value. As a salesperson, it's your job to discover the real value and pass this information to your prospects and customers.

I would like to leave you with a quote from our good friend Emerson, who said, "Nothing great was ever achieved without enthusiasm." So, if you're going to be great, you are going to have to get enthusiastic, wouldn't you agree?

ATTITUDE

Although it is not directly passion or enthusiasm, your attitude is a part of this excitement we are talking about. I would like to take a minute to discuss the right attitude and how your attitude can help you tremendously in your selling.

If you had to choose one word to describe the key to selling, I guess *attitude* would be the best choice. Almost every sales author I have read has talked about how you have to have a "proper attitude" if you want to succeed in selling. It is my belief that this is even more critical to success on the telephone because you don't have other visual aids to assist you in coloring your message.

Your telephone call is completely dependent on your voice for its power. Unfortunately, our vocal projection is tied very closely to how we feel at the moment. Take, for example, answering the phone when you have been awakened by the call. Nine times out of ten, the caller's first words to you after you say hello are, "Oh, I'm sorry, did I wake you?" Or, when you're not feeling well, the caller seems to discover this almost instantaneously. Because we project our feelings in our voice, this is natural.

Since attitude is so important, I would like to cover its implications and show how even the most remote relationships with your feelings can affect your calls and your success.

Do Salespeople Have Thick Skin, or Just Attitude?

Many people think salespeople have a thick skin because they seem to be able to take rejection so well. This may be the case, but I think this ability is more a part of a proper sales attitude.

The first part of a proper attitude is, of course, a positive approach. Without being positive it is very hard to sell successfully. The second, and more important, part is to realize that you're not going to get along with everyone. Even the best salespeople run into people with whom they can't strike up a successful relationship. They handle this by realizing that it takes a lot of noes to get a sale. Understanding this, they can thank the person who says no and move that much closer to their next sale. Third, being a successful salesperson requires you to have confidence, maybe even exaggerated confidence. Without the belief that something can be done, the effort needed to accomplish the task vanishes. We all know that without an effort, nothing happens. Thus, only the salesperson who believes the sales will come makes the consistent effort.

Because of the nature of the telephone selling environment and the ease with which prospects can terminate your effort, these three attitude factors are even more important.

To be successful you must:

1. Accept the idea that sales is a numbers game.
2. Know that you won't sell everyone.
3. Believe that you will make sales.

These are critically important because each is capable of spoiling your enthusiasm, thus destroying your attitude, and that will be transmitted over the telephone.

23

WORK HABITS

Does your attitude affect your work habits? Do your work habits affect your success on the telephone? They do! As we all know, success in selling can be simply reduced to numbers. It's no secret that the more calls you make, the more sales you will get, no matter what your skill level. Someone who has a bad attitude is likely not to make as many calls as someone with a good one.

More important to your telephone success, however, is the fact that your mind responds better when it is not filled with negative emotions. A bad attitude indicates that negative emotions are probably present. These emotions will affect the clarity of your thought process, making it more difficult for you to respond properly in given situations. The point has been made that in a gunfight, the person who is calm and collected has a tremendous advantage. This is true in a telephone sales presentation as well. If you get rattled or stumped, your emotional changes or hesitation can cause you to lose control of the call and your prospect. If your prospect is not completely on track with you, this may be just the moment when he or she decides to end the call.

What Have We Learned?

- The telephone transmits emotions perfectly.
- Using the three jewels of the phone, energy, enthusiasm, and passion, you will transmit the energy and motivation necessary to help your prospect make the buying decision.
- Only with belief that you can succeed will you make the proper effort.
- The better your attitude, the more calls you'll probably make.

The Second Rule of Telephone Selling

- Without energy, enthusiasm, and passion, you will not interest your prospects in your products. Never make a call without them.

Chapter Three Challenge

Discover what you sound like when you're truly excited about something. This may require you to carry a tape recorder around or use one on your phone calls to find a conversation that contains real excitement. Examine that call or situation carefully to discover what your excitement sounds like. This is the sound or tone you need to duplicate in your telephone sales presentations, if you want to be successful.

Develop a good attitude. Find reasons to be confident in what you do and positive about your company and its products. This can be done by digging out the real values your company and its products provide (see Practice).

Practice

1. Analyze and develop your ability to convey enthusiasm and energy in your presentation. Practice on tape to make sure your smile shows through when you speak in your presentation voice. Have a friend or coworker listen to your presentation to assure you of your enthusiastic tone.
2. Make a list of your company's key assets, those most valuable to the customer.
3. Make a list of the best reasons a customer might buy your products or services.
4. Solidify in your mind, by writing down, your reasons for being enthusiastic and passionate about your company's products or services.

[Sample answers to these exercises appear in the Appendix.]

Hints for Improving

There are a number of things you can do in this area to improve your calls. Use the following hints to help you improve.

1. Don't make calls when you cannot generate the proper positive energy.
2. Make calls in concentrated and focused sessions. If you dedicate a period of time for your calls (provided this is possible in your work environment), you will find that you can get in the swing, so to speak, and your calls will be of higher quality.
3. Take frequent breaks to get your mind clear and rested so that you can come back full steam. Do this if you have had a bad call or if you start to feel as if you have lost your edge. Even a short break will help you get going again.
4. Always avoid using your casual voice when presenting. Pay attention to how you sound during your call and make the appropriate corrections as you go.
5. Taping your calls and listening to them will give you great feedback. You don't need to be a trainer to hear many things that will improve your presentation greatly.
6. Learn to listen to yourself as you present with one question in mind: Is this call fun and interesting? If it's not, figure out how to change its tone. Look at it this way: If the call is already bad, you have very little to lose no matter what action you take.

Coming Up

In the next chapter I discuss your voice. As is obvious from our investigation so far, your voice is one of the most important factors in your success on the telephone.

FOUR

VOICE: YOUR PRIMARY WEAPON

WHAT IS THE DIFFERENCE BETWEEN
A CASUAL AND A PRESENTATION VOICE?

Our most significant problem with the telephone will always be old habits. For the first twenty or so years of our lives, we probably used the telephone extensively in a nonpersuasive environment. In our conversations with relatives, friends, and businesses, we were not required to persuade or influence others. Also, for the most part, we were not imposing on the person we were calling, as we often are in a telephone sales call. Our relatives and friends, and businesspeople who see us as potential customers, are willing and eager to talk with us. Yes, we have all experienced situations in which we were trying to influence friends and family, but the bulk of the time we spent on the telephone was, shall we say, *casual.* These casual calls required no special emphasis, and thus we never really learned to use any. In fact, through many years of casual conversation, we learned specifically *not* to use it, and this is the problem.

Casual Voice

This gives us the term *casual voice.* Your casual voice is the voice you use for telephone communication in the normal course of daily life. Here, of course, we are speaking specifically of the telephone; however, most of us use the same voice for the telephone that we use in person. Your casual voice rarely requires the transmission of emotion, but usually contains some form of it. As we discussed earlier, whether you like it or not, you typically transmit emotions or feelings almost with the first word from your mouth. *Presentation voice,* on the other hand, requires a calculated transmission of certain feelings and emotions, as we have already discussed. For the average person, a presentation voice is not natural; even after twenty-plus years of practice, sometimes it's still damned unnatural. We are so used to our natural emotions being the desirable transmission that we forget that when selling, our natural state may not be positive enough to support and motivate the customer to make the buying decision.

As with the commercials we discussed in Chapter 2, on the

telephone people judge you almost immediately, deciding very quickly what value you might have for them and whether or not they want to listen to you. If you think about receiving sales calls at home, you will realize that you, too, quickly make this same judgment when someone calls. You will find that even if you naturally cut such calls short, on occasion you will engage the person on the other end of the line in a real conversation. This happens when you make the instant judgment that that person's value is different. You will also find that it is not the person's products that causes this to happen, but the person's approach and the gut feeling you get that makes the biggest difference. For example, if you get a call and make the decision that this is a really nice person on the other end of the phone, your reaction will be completely different from that when you answer and hear the caller reading a script.

THE DANGERS OF YOUR CASUAL VOICE

By now it should be obvious that you must be selling with your voice when you make telephone presentations. This means creating a tone that will move the prospects in the direction you want them to go. You will not be using your casual voice, as your casual voice isn't normally moving (creating emotional change), it's neutral. In general, there is nothing wrong with being neutral, but in a sales presentation it is not persuasive and is often boring, and being boring is not going to help you win customers. You will typically find that your casual voice often lacks three key ingredients to winning your prospects.

1. *Energy*—to get the prospect excited
2. *Enthusiasm*—to get the prospect's attention and motivate him or her
3. *Confidence*—to show the prospect you are a knowledgeable professional

To sell effectively on the telephone, you must use a presentation voice at all times. This is true not just because of the transmission of feeling you wish to achieve, but for some practical reasons as well. To understand this better, let's briefly examine the presentation voice in more detail.

Presentation Voice

A good presentation voice includes first and foremost the three jewels, energy, enthusiasm, and passion. These three facets of your telephone presentation are critically important. It is your energy and enthusiasm that create the proper mood for the prospect. There are other factors to this presentation voice that will aid you as well:

1. Volume
2. Enunciation
3. Pronunciation
4. Vocabulary
5. Speed of delivery

Volume

The volume you use on the telephone is very important. Although the telephone is a great transmitter of emotion and attitude, it is often a difficult medium for the transmission of data. There are a couple of factors that make your volume important, the first being line quality. As you are well aware, sometimes you get a phone line that is just not that good quality. There can be static or noise on the line, and you can sometimes have fade or drop-out in the transmission, making the volume of either voice too low to hear easily. Since you want the prospect concentrating on your presentation, the last thing you need is a line that forces her or him to work just to hear you.

The second factor making your volume important is the prospect's environment. Since you can't see the prospect's environment during your call, it is important to realize that any number of things may be going on around him or her that make it more difficult to hear. There may be others on the telephone nearby, a maintenance person outside the window with a blower, or a copier repairperson working in the office.

By maintaining a good volume in your calls, you decrease the need for the prospect to work just to hear you. In addition, a bit more volume supports your effort to project an energetic and enthusiastic tone. Volume also gives you the sound of authority and confidence. The correct volume for your phone calls is probably about the same as you would use to talk to a small group in a meeting. Using such a volume not only makes it easier for the prospect to hear you, but improves the way you sound to the prospect as well.

Enunciation

We have all had the experience, when talking to someone on the telephone, of trying to get the spelling of that person's name or his or her street address, and finding it almost impossible to understand what the person was saying. This is a frustration you don't need to give your prospect. For this reason, you need to pay special attention to your enunciation of words during your telephone presentation. In this way you increase your prospect's ability to understand what you are saying.

Unfortunately, many people simply won't ask about what they don't hear. They feel it's rude to ask you to repeat, or maybe they think they know what you said and just never ask you to confirm their understanding. If you're not careful, you can get all the way to the end of your presentation and find out the prospect missed a key point. This ruins the flow of your presentation and thus endangers your ability to make the sale.

One way to avoid possible misunderstandings is to ask frequent questions in your presentation that confirm what you are saying. You might say, *Does that all make sense to you, Ms. Prospect?* or *Do you have any questions so far?*

Pronunciation

Pronunciation is the other half of saying words clearly. Pronunciation is also a factor in the image you present to the prospect. Educated people pronounce words correctly, whereas less educated people may not. Professional people are known for their good communications skills, and you wouldn't expect to hear sloppy pronunciation in their speech.

By making sure that both your enunciation and your pronunciation are good, you will project the image of a true professional. Even though you may not be an expert, it is easier for the prospect to see you in that light if your speech is clear and concise.

Vocabulary

If you listen to radio, you have probably heard many commercials for vocabulary tapes. Many people use your vocabulary to judge your level of education, which is often equated with your professionalism or expertise. This is not necessarily done consciously; it is often done subconsciously and is processed by the brain as a feeling about the person on the other end of the line.

Being careful with your vocabulary and avoiding slang is always a good idea. In addition, you may want to practice choosing your words carefully to make the best impression you can on your prospects and customers. Remember, the telephone doesn't have the visual advantages of a face-to-face meeting— every little bit of help you can get in creating the best image of yourself for the prospect is important.

Especially if you are just starting your sales career, you might find that the purchase and use of such tapes greatly enhances your progress.

One other factor in vocabulary is product-related idioms and terminology—for example, in the computer industry, terms like ROM and RAM, or in financial services, annuity and ROI. You must learn the language of your industry and its products. In fact, this is a good way to understand the real benefits of the products. Knowing the terms often lets you know what is important to the prospect about a particular product or service.

Speed of Delivery

One of the questions most frequently asked by attendees of my seminars is, "How fast should I go?" Apart from the technique of using speed for emphasis, speed is really a function of the prospect's understanding of your presentation. The key to your delivery speed is making sure the prospect is comprehending what you say. A controlled, deliberate speed seems to work best for me. The best analogy to this would be the way in which news anchors present their stories.

Another technique used by many salespeople is to match the prospect's speed. Since people usually speak at a comfortable data rate, you can use that rate to communicate with them. It is probably prudent not to use a speed that is uncomfortable to you, so as to avoid causing yourself a distraction in your presentation. Whatever speed you choose, you should be completely comfortable in your presentation or your discomfort will be transmitted to your prospect.

One other important point about speed needs to be made, that is, being rushed by the prospect or customer. Never allow the prospect or customer to force you into rushing your information. If the prospect seems rushed or wants you to rush, you should investigate the opportunity to call back at a more convenient time. Rushing your presentation will only get you in trouble.

THINGS THAT GO BUMP IN YOUR VOICE

Confidence

There are a couple of items, some of which we discussed earlier, that are critical to your vocal presentation. The first of these is confidence. Confidence is a part of your attitude and a necessary part of your presentation, especially in the tougher calls. If you are not confident, prospects will end up with control of the call, making it significantly more difficult to close the deal. When you talk to people on the telephone, you will find that some seem mousy while others simply run you over with their controlling nature. The best solution to sounding confident is to really *be* confident. If you have real confidence, it will be projected over the telephone.

You may have had, as I have, the experience of working for a company that was far better at promising than at delivering.

This can make you nervous when you close the sale, as you begin to wonder if the company will really deliver what you promised. In this case, you may not have real confidence, and thus some acting is required. Confidence can be projected in a number of simple ways. The first is the volume of your voice. The casual voice is well known for its lack of projection of confidence. The primary reason for this is the volume. Turn up your volume on the telephone and you begin to sound more confident. This almost always happens automatically when you remember the three jewels: energy, enthusiasm, and passion.

The second part of confidence comes from the way in which you phrase your sentences. Certain phrases just reek of a person who's not sure of him- or herself. For example:

If you don't mind, could I speak to the VP?
Better: *May I speak to the VP, please.*

I'm not really sure how that works.
Better: *I don't know the answer to that, but I will find out and give you a call back.*

If you decide you want to get the widget, you can give me a call.
Better: *Once you decide, call me and I will get you set up.*

The major difference in these phrases is the addition of an unnecessary qualification or statement to the real objective. In the first statement, for example, the qualification *If you don't mind* is not confident, whereas asking politely and firmly to speak to the VP says, "I'm important, and it is necessary for me to reach this person." It is especially important to look for these statements in your closes. Most salespeople get soft when it comes to asking the closing question, as in the third statement above. It's much more confident to assume that the order is coming and direct the prospect what to do, rather than tell him or her *if*—then you'll take the order. We will deal with this in more detail in Chapter 9.

One of the best measures of your confidence is the amount of resistance put up by screens. Screens are secretaries, receptionists, and others who initially answer the phone. If you find yourself being grilled by these people, it is quite possible that your presentation lacks confidence. This screening is also a common result of someone using a very low volume. If you don't sound as if you are in control, others will treat you as if they are! This is not limited to screens; it includes your prospects and customers.

Smile

The other thing you must watch for in your voice is its smile. It is quite easy to lose the smile in your voice when talking to a prospect, especially in a longer call, or when the call has a lot of technical issues that must be discussed. You must constantly remind yourself to smile when you are on the telephone, and make sure that there is a smile in your voice. The only way to get a smile on someone's face is to smile at that person or tell a joke. Since you are on the phone, you must make sure that the smile on your face is in your voice. Telling jokes is OK but probably not a practical approach to telephone selling.

VOCAL TACTICS

There are a number of things you can do with your voice that assist you in your presentation. Also, there are things you do with your voice that can cause problems. Let's examine these factors one at a time.

Pausing and Skipping

Pausing is an effective technique that can be used for a number of purposes. By pausing you can emphasize a point.

> *Your biggest benefit . . . from our program, Ms. Prospect, is that you will receive . . . A . . . and B . . . , which are specifically what you were looking for.*

The pauses after *benefit* and *receive* accent the "good" to the prospect. By pausing after the actual benefits, A and B, we emphasize those features. This helps to make them more important to the prospect and helps get the prospect focused on them.

Of course, the reverse is true as well. If you pause after the price, you emphasize that price, which may not be your intention. When you want to deemphasize a particular point, you can do what is called *skipping*. This is where you surround the point to be deemphasized with emphasis on other points, moving slightly more quickly through the deemphasized area. For example:

> *Your biggest benefit . . . from our program, Ms. Prospect, is that you will receive . . . A . . . and B . . . || for just $299.95 over the five years you participate in the program, || and of course you will receive A . . . and B . . . , which are specifically the benefits you were looking for.*

You would give this presentation at normal speed up to the bars (| |), at which point you would go just slightly faster until you finished the price statement, when you would slow down once again. This focuses all of the prospect's attention on the big benefits and decreases the emphasis on the actual price. This is a good strategy for answering the tougher questions about your products or services. Try to surround the answer with positive statements to deemphasize the effect. Use the pause to emphasize the good points and move promptly through the more negative part of the answer.

Another key point regarding pauses is that you must be careful where you pause in the natural flow of your conversation on the telephone. Pauses at the end of statements, or after answers to prospect questions, are often invitations for your prospect to ask another question. It is not bad that the prospect asks questions, but it is better if you are in control of the call. We will discuss call control later in the book, but for now just know that this can cause a distraction in your presentation by interrupting the flow of information and of your presentation of the critical material.

Speed Changes

In talking about pauses, we have already mentioned changing speed. You can help to emphasize a point by slowing down your presentation of that point as well as deemphasize it by speeding up. You can also use speed changes to help the prospect understand complicated or critical information in your presentation.

Trail-Offs

You will probably need your recorder to discover your affinity for trail-offs. Most of us don't catch this very important aspect of our discussion with prospects. A trail-off is where your voice drops out at the end of your sentence, sort of like this:

You already have a widget?

These answers very often sound like questions. They are also audible signs of disappointment in your voice. Most people don't pay a lot of attention to them, but my experience is that they make a big difference because they usually come in the more critical selling situations.

Their natural tendency is to present a feeling of "the end," "finality," or that the situation is hopeless and no further discussion is necessary. Depending on the circumstances of the call, trail-offs can come across as indicating that you have nothing left to say after that answer. When this happens, you may find that the prospect quickly concludes the call for you without giving you a chance to investigate further. Let me give you an excellent example from my own consulting practice. Like most businesses, I advertise in the Yellow Pages. However, a large portion of my calls are from people who are seeking a service bureau. I have on occasion given an answer to this question without my usual enthusiasm and found my caller quickly on the way to the next call in the search. I discovered quite quickly, however, that if I make a more positive statement without the trail-off of disappointment, I find that I can continue the call. In a recent call this turned out to be quite profitable. After explaining in a positive way that I was not a service bureau, I was able to investigate the prospect's real interest. If I had not done this, I would have lost a major opportunity, as the caller was trying to compare the service bureau route to setting up an internal program. Because I was able to continue the conversation positively, I had the opportunity to win the business. A trail-off in this situation might have ended the call.

All things have both a positive and negative side, and trail-offs are no exception. You can use the disappointed tone and the trail-off to your advantage when discussing the competition. (This takes a little finesse or you may come across as phony.) For example, you might give the competitor a compliment while at the same time using the trail-off to show your lack of confidence.

Yes, I'm sure ACB is a good company . . . but we . . .

The first part of the statement is in your casual voice, and you go back to a presentation voice as you change to yourself.

Hammering

Hammering is the process of hitting a word or phrase with a bit more emphasis, usually done with volume—for example, in the phrase:

. . . and it's just $14.95 per month . . .

In this example you might hammer, or emphasize, the word *just* in order to emphasize the coming price.

The object of all these techniques is to give you a voice that is alive and energetic. You don't want to be monotone or boring—you will just put the prospect to sleep. The object is to convey your own positive feelings to the prospect to aid him or her in the decision-making process. The more fun the prospect has on the call, the more likely you will be to get a relationship from which you can close a sale.

YOUR BREATH AND VOCAL TONE

Another aspect of your voice is its tone. You don't have a lot of direct control over the tonal qualities in your voice, unless you resort to voice lessons. However, there is one major factor in tone that you can control, thus improving the tonal qualities of your voice: breath.

You will find that as you get excited or emotional, your breath changes. These changes in your breath are responsible for many of the changes in your voice. If we listen to the Eastern sages, we learn that the breath is the central control and primary core of our nature. In other words, it reflects our emotional and physical states. Additionally, we discover that when we control our breath, we can control our physical and mental states as well.

When making your telephone presentation, you want to keep your breathing full and steady. This will keep you calm and clear-minded and give your voice a deeper, more aesthetic sound.

I unfortunately learned about breathing during my presentations the hard way. My first encounter with telephone selling was to consumers. Because I was nervous, I tended not to breathe at all during our short script, and by the end of the presentation, my voice had gone up by a couple of octaves. In addition, by the time I was ready to ask for the order, I needed another breath to refresh my depleted oxygen supply. This led to a situation in which prior to my closing question, the prospect heard this gasp for air, and after the gasp I usually heard the dial tone. So learn to breathe calmly and fully and it will help your presentation, and remember that when you get flustered or upset during your call, you can use your breathing to put you back on track.

A SIMPLE METHOD FOR IMPROVING

Unfortunately, through the medium of print it is impossible to give examples of how these techniques actually sound. However, you can learn these and others by watching and listening to professional speakers. If you want to learn how to present a professional image, listen to the major news anchors. If you want to learn how to use emotion in your presentation, listen to the evangelists. You will also find lots of "infomercials" on your cable channels that may give you presentation ideas. Finally, remember to pay attention to how media commercials achieve their objectives. Listen to the way commercials for different products use the announcer's voice to achieve different effects.

Make tapes of your calls and compare your performance to that of the professionals you have been listening to in the media. This is especially effective for general speaking techniques such as projection, enunciation, pronunciation, volume, and speed. You can hear for yourself if your prospect is talking with you, rather than at you. You should hear your smile and confidence.

Bringing It Together

You don't need a fabulous voice. Most of us don't have that special voice that all the advertisers are searching for. We just have normal voices, imperfect in many ways compared to broadcasting standards.

What you do need is to sound like a professional, to have credibility, and to be fun to talk to. Professionalism comes from speaking clearly and using an appropriate vocabulary. Credibility comes from your own confidence and belief in yourself, your company, and the products you sell. As for being fun to talk to, you must have energy and a smile in your voice. In other words, you need to sound as if you have a personality, not monotone or uninterested in your own presentation.

It's Not So Much What You Say as How You Say It

Experience has taught me that it is not so much what you say as how you say it. People buy from people. The relationship you forge in your conversation is probably more important than anything else in making the sale. If someone is your "friend," he or she is much more likely to buy from you.

Having fun on the telephone isn't just necessary to maintain your sanity, it's good business. Making friends makes making customers much easier. This is one of the reasons you want to have an exciting and enthusiastic presentation: Without it you will have trouble getting the prospect excited about what it is you're doing.

Friends listen better. As you know, it's easier to talk to one of your friends than to most prospects. This is true because of the comfort level you have developed. By having an enjoyable conversation with your prospect, you decrease the distance and begin to form a relationship with that person. This is the beginning of the development of trust.

You will find that the prospects that you have fun with on the telephone are the ones who want to talk to you on the second call. My personal experience is that most of the people I call back are very happy to hear from me, even when they still cannot use my products. Also, I find that people remember me for quite a long period of time after the first call. This is a sign that I have made an impression, that I have in some way started a relationship.

Whenever you are in a telephone sales situation, you should constantly ask yourself the question, "Is this call fun?" If you are having a good time, the chances are that your prospect is, too. If you are finding the call difficult, it is quite possible that your prospect or customer is also not feeling all that well. You must, in these situations, take immediate action to change the direction of the call. You can add more energy to your presentation, you can ask the prospect about his or her business—there are any number of things you can try. The important thing is to make an effort to improve the tone of the call and move it to a more "fun" environment.

What Have We Learned?

- We have two telephone voices, a casual one and an emphasized one, our presentation voice.
- Our casual voice has low impact (emotionally).
- We must present in our high-impact presentation voice at all times.
- The keys to a good presentation voice are volume, enunciation, pronunciation, vocabulary, speed, and of course the three jewels, energy, enthusiasm, and passion.

- There are two critical components of our voice we must be careful to maintain, confidence and a smile.
- Vocal quality can be improved by proper breathing.
- Key vocal tactics are pausing and skipping, trail-offs, and hammering.

Practice

1. Use your recorder to record a number of normal conversations, then record a number of sales calls. Listen to your tape and compare your casual voice to your presentation voice.
2. Now reread the chapter, making notes regarding the things you need to improve in your presentation voice as you go.
3. Write out the answers to a couple of the primary objections you encounter in your sales presentation, then present those answers to your recorder using your notes as a guide to improve your presentation voice.
4. Repeat this process a couple of times. After each repetition, take some time to listen to a professional presenter (motivational speaker, news anchor, evangelist). As you listen to these people, think about what they are doing with their voice for effect, and see how they use vocal tactics to influence the audience.
5. One of the key things you must do in your presentations is to avoid losing your energy or enthusiasm, even when the going gets tough on the phone. This was the reason I suggested you write out some of the key objectives. Try at this point to come up with some other negative situations, then write out your answers and use them to practice your presentation voice.

[Sample ideas for these exercises appear in the Appendix.]

Hints for Improving

1. Make sure every call is energized by your enthusiasm and passion for what you do.
2. Check your energy before each call.
3. Don't rush your presentation for anyone. If a prospect doesn't have time, reschedule the call for another time.
4. Take full breaths, even deep ones, when presenting. It will give you better vocal tone.
5. Learn by audiotaping your presentation and listening for opportunities to improve.

FIVE

NERDs AND THE DECISION MAKER

What Is a Nerd?

No, I'm not talking about the skinny little guy with the thick glasses, pocket calculator, and a pocket holder full of pens. In sales a NERD is a person *N*ot *E*mpowered to *R*ender a *D*ecision. In other words, this person cannot make a buying decision.

This doesn't mean you can treat this person like dirt. In fact, you must be extra careful how you attend to this individual— first, because you don't know who you're talking to, and second, because you want information, and even though this individual may not be part of the decision-making process, he or she may know who is, and that's information you need.

Let me relay a true story about the handling of NERDs from my own experience. Recently I worked with a software company in which the president's wife often took incoming telephone calls if the receptionist was busy or away from her desk. She was basically her husband's executive assistant, handling a number of key tasks for him. One day a salesperson, I believe from a communications company, called, and the president's wife answered the phone. This salesperson had called a couple of times before and had run into a problem that even the company's employees had, and that was finding the president available to chat. Being frustrated, and feeling that he was getting the runaround, the salesperson got a bit rude and belligerent with the woman who answered the phone, not knowing that she was the president's wife. After a bit of squabbling she put the salesperson on hold and told her husband, the president, about this character on the phone. He took the call. After the president answered the phone, the salesperson introduced himself and began his presentation, at which point the president stopped him and asked the following question: "Why would I want to do business with someone who feels it's all right to mistreat my employees, specifically my wife, when he calls?" There was a brief silence and the president hung up the telephone.

Remember, you are blind when you call a prospect company. You usually don't have a clue as to the relationships of the individuals involved. It is possible, and likely, that people other than the receptionist or secretary may at times answer the phone. If you mistake these people for reception staff and mistreat them, you may be in for a real surprise later on when you find out how important they are to the decision maker. Although these persons would be considered by our definition NERDs, they represent a potential resource, and if mishandled, a probable disaster. Treat them like gold.

BE CAREFUL WITH YOUR ASSUMPTIONS

Many people on the reception staff have mastered the art of sounding like a decision maker. In addition, other people in the organization, and possibly in the decision loop, may also answer your call. Never make the assumption that they are decision makers without qualifying them, a subject we will cover in detail in the next chapter.

You must be especially careful of who answers the telephone, *I can help you!* Often people who answer the phone in this way are designated screens. They may know of a particular project or task with the organization and have specific instructions to screen those calls.

NERDS CAN BE A GREAT SOURCE OF INFORMATION

It's not that you don't want to talk to NERDs, it's just that you don't want to present to them. Making a presentation to a NERD can be dangerous, as we will see in a minute.

To an outsider, NERDs have one very valuable commodity, knowledge of the organization. In many cases you will not know who's who in the companies you prospect, but the NERD might! This can be very valuable.

There are a number of things you can do with NERDs that will greatly assist you in your sales effort. Here are just a few.

1. Get the name of the decision maker.
2. Confirm an individual's authority.
3. Learn about the company.
4. Learn about the decision-making process.
5. Find out about the competition.

Of course, it depends on what level NERD you get. The receptionist may not have the information you want, whereas a department secretary or administrator or other personnel in the decision maker's group may.

SOME NERDs ARE VERY IMPORTANT!

Personal administrators, receptionists, assistants, and secretaries are very important to your success. In my own business, I add these names to my database and use them often when calling to find the decision maker. For example, I might find out that Ann is the administrator for Fred, the vice president of sales. I will add Ann's name to my database, indicating her relationship to Fred. Then when I call Fred and I get a female voice, I make the assumption and start my sentence *Ann?* Most of the time I'm right, and now Ann is very appreciative of my treatment of her. In fact, I often develop great relationships with the decision makers' assistants and administrators long before I actually speak to the decision makers themselves.

Cultivation of these types of relationships is crucial to prospecting success and extremely helpful to any sales effort. After a time, these individuals start to feed me little tidbits of information that are extremely useful in finding the decision maker. In many cases they keep me informed of the decision maker's schedule, how busy the decision maker is, if the decision maker is in a good mood, or the response to my inquiry or to information I might have mailed before I reached the decision maker. All of this information adds up to a better chance of reaching the right person successfully.

THE PITFALLS OF PRESENTING TO NERDs

The NERD Can't Buy

The largest and most obvious pitfall is that you can't ever hope to make the sale. If your responsibility is to sell, then you are hopelessly lost to start with when you present to a NERD. As we have already mentioned, it's not that you don't want to talk with a NERD, it's just that you don't want to spend your time presenting to him or her. But this, although a logical reason, is by far not the only pitfall of presenting to NERDs.

Clinging to the Wrong Needs

In most cases you will find that the NERD is not fully knowledgeable about the true needs of the decision maker. It is my supposition that only by talking to the decision maker can you discover his or her true needs and their relative importance. If you make your presentation to a NERD, you may be guided into supporting needs that are of lower value more fully and possibly not supporting the most critical needs of the decision maker at all. NERDs may not interpret the decision maker's needs in the same way he or she does. This goes for understanding as well as value.

A NERD may have his or her own agenda or personal biases. In a situation involving a high-technology product such as a computer, an engineer who is a user of the products you are selling may have a viewpoint concerning what is critical to the system to be purchased that is different from that of the actual decision maker. What's important isn't whether the NERD's view is right or wrong, but how that view aligns with the decision maker's. If the views don't align, the supports you create for your sale may be in the wrong places, causing it to crumble in front of the decision maker.

This situation is very much akin to making a sales presentation to a child whose parents are going to make the product purchase. It's true that the child has some say in what will be purchased; however, the parents are going to make certain decisions with regard to the purchase that may not be in line with the child's wild desires. Focusing your presentation on the satisfaction of the child's desires without consideration of the parents' may quickly frustrate the parents, who then remove the child, possibly against his or her will, and search somewhere else for the product.

Losing the Decision Maker's Ear

One of the most deadly situations you can become involved with in your sales effort is being fenced off from the decision maker. This can happen in a number of ways, but it usually occurs through making presentations to NERDs. The consumer example of this is probably most striking, and certainly most memorable in the minds of those like myself who sold for so long to consumers. The conversation goes like this:

Salesperson:	*Hello. This is Ms. Salesperson with ABC Company. Is the lady of the house available?*
Daughter:	*How can I help you?*
Salesperson:	*Well, we are the company that helps households . . . (and so on about her product).*
Daughter:	*Just a minute. Let me get my mom.*
Salesperson:	*OK.*
Daughter:	*(yelling across the house): Mom, there is a woman from ABC Company selling . . . do you want to talk to her?*
Mom:	*What's it about?*
Daughter:	*What are you selling?*
Salesperson:	*ABC manufactures widgets . . .*
Daughter:	*Mom, they sell widgets.*
Mom:	*No, tell 'em I'm not interested.*
Daughter:	*She says she's not interested, thanks.*

This particular situation leaves the salesperson no recourse on the objection *I'm not interested.* You can bet that the daughter's tone when she tells her mom about the salesperson's products is less than enthusiastic when she is just waiting for her boyfriend to call.

For the salesperson, this is a wasted call. She's lost a prospect without ever having the chance to present. The cause of this predicament was the salesperson's diving into the presentation at the beginning of the call, before making sure she had the proper person on the telephone.

In a business-to-business call, there are actually more ways in which you can be blocked from the decision maker. The first is the secretary or administrator of the decision maker. This person has usually been given instructions on how to handle certain types of calls. If you make your presentation to this individual, you can quickly be put in the position of waiting for the decision maker's call, thus losing your ability to expedite and pursue the action you desire. Once the screen believes that he or she understands what you want, he or she will feel obligated to protect the decision maker with the statement *She will call you if she's interested.*

The second problem occurs with people who are involved in the process, but do not have the authority to make decisions. As we discuss in the chapter on qualifying, sometimes these individuals are part of the decision process and necessary steps on the road to the final decision maker. However, when they are not, making a presentation to them can be a disaster. Two things can now happen to your ability to make the presentation to the decision maker. First, this person can forward the material to the decision maker; then, when you call, the decision maker gives you the response, *I have your materials; I'll call you if I'm interested.* Second, you can get stuck with the screen, who now won't give you the name of the decision maker and continues to give you the same response: *He will call you if he's interested.*

In all of the above cases, you have lost the chance at the decision maker's ear. Now the presentation of your product or service is dependent on a third party. This brings on a number of new problems.

THE THIRD-PARTY PRESENTER

The third party knows less about your products than you do, can't answer critical questions, and is probably far less enthusiastic about your products than you would be. All of these factors decrease your ability to make a sale, and in many cases your ability to present your products.

However, the biggest factors are the relationships developed and the presentation quality.

Relationships

I think it's pretty easy to agree that creating quality relationships is the key to making sales. You're not going to sell to someone without first having a good relationship with that person. If you never talk to the decision maker, it is difficult to develop a relationship with her or him. In this case, you must depend on your relationship with the third party. Unfortunately, this involves a lot of luck.

There is considerably more stress in the relationship between you and a third party in the sales process than there would be between you and the decision maker. This stress comes from your constant reference to the decision maker in your need to understand the solution. As much as you try to work with the third party, there is always that tone of *I really need to talk to the decision maker*. This puts stress on the call. Another stress provider is the fact that the third party often doesn't have all the answers necessary for the process to run smoothly. Thus, you often end up in situations where many extra calls are necessary for the process to be completed, because the third party has to go find information necessary to the process.

Presentation Quality

Working through a third party also gives you the problem that the individual who is now giving your presentation to the decision maker may not be capable, or desirous, of making the same presentation you would. The third party is not likely to present your product or service with any significant amount of enthusiasm. Also, as already mentioned, the third party will not have the product or solution knowledge level that you have and would be able to present. This means that he or she won't be able to answer questions or deal with changes in the direction of the desired solution as you would.

Because you lack direct access to the decision maker's needs and desires, you don't have the ability to adjust your presentation to cover the things that most concern the decision maker. This weakens your presentation.

The Ability to Close

Finally, and probably most important, you can't close. Unless the third party has some vested interest in your solution, he or she is not likely to pursue the decision to buy your product. There will not be any trial closing, which is essential for the development of the proper solution through the handling of objections.

In summary, NERDs are most likely going to waste your time and impede your ability to sell, although they have uses, such as being an information source. However, they must be treated carefully and with respect. Like it or not, although they don't have the authority to make a decision, they do have the ability to negatively affect the decision being made or to hinder your effort to get a fair hearing for your company and its products.

WHO IS THE DECISION MAKER?

This almost sounds like a silly question, but there is more to understanding your decision maker than you might think. It's true that the decision maker is the person who can say yes to the order, but it is often much more complicated than that. In order to have the best chance of making the sale, you need to know the decision-making capabilities of the person you're presenting to.

Although we talk more about this in the chapter on qualifying, it is important to mention here that often prospects will mislead you as to their real decision-making authority. You must be extremely careful not to be fooled by NERDs who attempt to impersonate the decision maker.

Different Sales, Different Decision Makers

It is important to note that each product or service has its typical decision makers. Whatever your industry, you must discover who these people are. Is the decision maker the president of the company, the MIS manager, the controller, or the office manager? It depends on your product and the type of customers you deal with.

In many cases business decisions are made by more than one person. For example, a company wishing to buy computers may involve the MIS manager to decide which computers are necessary and what brand should be purchased. However, the controller may be involved in the budgetary considerations, and the president of the company may sign off on the entire transaction.

So who is the decision maker? In this example, they all are. The key is to talk with the person in primary control of the decision. In this case, it would probably be the MIS manager, as he or she is the one who understands the needs of the organization and can choose the quality level of the machines to be purchased. Of course, you must confirm this, as it is possible that the decision is being made on budgetary grounds or that the president has a favorite vendor.

Often the decisions require the review of considerable information. Companies frequently take an individual who is extremely knowledgeable about the decision at hand and give him or her the job of evaluating the company's options, and then making a recommendation. For example, a large company may wish to purchase a medical plan. This is a significant decision and would probably not be made by just one person in the organization. In this instance, the company might take one of its key people from the HR department, one who has experience in medical plans, and assign him to reviewing the available plans. On the basis of his review, he would then make a recommendation to the decision committee. That committee might consist of the president, vice president, controller, and human resource manager. In this situation, although the person evaluating the material is not the final decision maker, he is the person whom you will have to sell. Your approach to this presentation may be different from your approach to a presentation made to the final decision maker in that you must sort out the needs of the evaluator and those of the decision committee.

WHY IS IT IMPORTANT TO TALK TO THE DECISION MAKER?

Although they are probably already clear, let's quickly review the key reasons for talking directly to the decision maker.

Only the decision maker can buy! Any selling effort made to someone who cannot buy is potentially a waste of time. If you don't have the decision maker on the phone, you can't close the deal. The person you are talking to must go to the decision maker and do that for you. In the case of the medical plan purchase, where the company used one of its people to evaluate and recommend the solution, you must sell that person on your solution as being the best. Your goal is to get him to recommend your product to the decision-making committee. In such a case, that is usually your only option.

Only the decision maker, or the decision-making team, really knows the reasons for buying. Dealing through any third party puts you, the seller, at risk of missing key information about the customer's desires. This makes it difficult to determine the best solution for that customer.

The quality of third-party presentations of your product will not be as good as yours. It is almost impossible to give a third party all the answers he or she may need in order to properly present your product to the decision maker. Furthermore, it is likely that the third party won't have the same excitement and enthusiasm for the product that you do. All of these factors of course reduce the power of your presentation.

Finally, the third party will not close the deal, but will ask for a decision. He or she will not go after the decision in the same way you would. The third party's relationship to the decision maker is very different. This often necessitates your eventually talking with the decision maker yourself to close the deal. At this point you will often have to repeat much of your presentation to the decision maker. It usually turns out that had you talked with the decision maker first, you could have saved considerable time and effort.

How Do You Identify the Decision Maker?

Although I discuss the qualification of the decision maker in more detail in the next chapter, on qualifying, I believe it is important to mention this process here.

Once you understand the importance of knowing your decision maker and his or her ability to buy, you have made a major step toward making the sale.

The best way to find your decision maker is to understand the decision process of the company to which you are selling. This knowledge is also useful in properly following the course of the sale. Your knowledge of the process helps you avoid stepping on toes and at the same time allows you to know what your options are based on where in the process you happen to be.

Ask the prospect how the decision to make this purchase will take place. What are the steps involved in the company's decision? Who are the parties involved, and what are their responsibilities? The answers to these questions are the key to your finding or identifying the person you should be talking to. These questions have a bonus byproduct in that they will quickly qualify the person you are talking to as a decision maker or non-decision maker.

Salespeople who haven't asked these questions before are astounded at the amount of information they receive. Once the prospect starts to tell you how the decision is made, he or she begins to reveal many valuable pieces of the puzzle you need to put together for your sale. You can very often tell by the answer exactly who makes the final decision. If the person you are speaking to has put himself or herself out of the loop, relative to a direct presentation, you will understand who you can talk to, and what that person's relationship to the purchasing decision is.

If you ask these questions early in the conversation, you will quickly qualify the person to whom you are speaking. This allows you to make choices in the direction of your call and your approach.

SUMMARY

In this chapter we have covered in detail the importance of the decision maker and her or his NERDs. You should now have a new respect for the value of discovering the right person before you make a sales presentation. Who is the true decision maker is often not clear-cut. You may talk to someone in the process who is not the decision maker but has some influence on the actual decision. Understanding this should give you the ability to compensate depending on the influence the person you talk to has on the decision process.

What Have We Learned?

- NERDs are important people and should be well treated, as they can be sources of valuable information.
- Assuming information about the responsibility of your prospect can be very dangerous.
- Presenting to NERDs can be very dangerous and misleading.
- Presenting to NERDs can lead to difficulties in reaching the decision maker.
- You must know the decision process if you want to be sure of your decision maker's authority.

Practice

1. Lay out the typical scenarios for the decision-making process in your business. This would include the titles and relationships of the decision makers you usually talk to. Set a plan for presenting to the different decision makers.
2. Develop a series of questions that will qualify the decision maker and the decision-making process for you.
3. Look for questions and statements you can use to avoid making a presentation to a NERD.

[Sample answers to these exercises appear in the Appendix.]

Hints for Improving

1. Practice gathering one good piece of information from the NERD before moving on. Any qualifying question that the NERD might answer is good.
2. Make a habit of asking about the decision-making process, so that you better understand the decision maker you're talking with.
3. Learn how to customize your presentation to deal with different levels of decision makers.

SIX

PROPER QUALIFYING

WHAT IS QUALIFYING?

Everybody knows you must qualify your prospect or customer before you make your presentation. Unfortunately, few salespeople are really effective at qualifying. The reason salespeople don't qualify well is the lack of good questioning technique and failing to understand what should be qualified. The typical salesperson will ask a prospect, *Are you the decision maker?* This question is not always effective in determining the real answer to the question. Often a gatekeeper will say in response, *I can help you.* Without further qualification, you won't make the discovery that you don't have the decision maker until you finish your presentation, at which point it's too late.

There are other things that should be qualified. Proper qualification involves qualifying all the critical tasks and issues within the sales presentation, not just determining if the person you are speaking to is the decision maker. Qualifying involves finding out if a company is a prospective buyer (can it use your product), confirming the decision maker's authority, closing all the "transactions" that take place in the call, and, most important, understanding the decision-making process. But good qualifying means much more, including qualifying prospect questions and objections. It also means discovering the underlying motivations and reasons for the prospect's requests for action by the salesperson, before turning cartwheels for the prospect.

THE NATURE OF QUALIFYING QUESTIONS

In the world of selling, *qualifying* could quite easily be interchanged with *understanding*. Qualifying in its true sense is understanding. In a sales situation, the primary purpose of qualifying is not the understanding itself, but the determination that a specific ingredient is present. For example, in trying to qualify the decision maker with the question, *How will your company make the decision to buy these widgets?* you are not necessarily that interested in the company's organization chart (although that information might be very helpful). However, you must make sure that the individual you're speaking with is indeed capable of making the decision you desire. Although the answers to qualifying questions usually turn out to have value later in the presentation, they are not the primary reason for the qualifying questions. This is probably why most salespeople have trouble doing a good job of qualification.

To understand how this works, let's look at a typical decision-maker qualification question: *Are you in charge of buying widgets for your company?* The common answer to this question is *Yes* or *I can help you.* At this point the salesperson usually continues with the presentation. Unfortunately, these answers do not necessary confirm that you have the decision maker on the phone. Let's compare the two questions to see the difference.

Asking a person directly if he or she is the decision maker may work some of the time; however, in many cases the person will tell you that he or she is the decision maker at first in order to understand what it is you're selling. Sometimes this person has been assigned the task of collecting information, or he or she may be involved in the decision-making process in some other way that causes him or her to be interested in what you might have to say. To many a salesperson's surprise, at the end of the presentation their prospect responds with, *This is great. I will forward this to the decision maker and have him call you if he is interested,* leaving the salesperson out in the cold.

The first question demands far more of the prospect and leaves less room for error. When we ask for the decision process, the prospect is forced to tell us the steps a product must go through to be purchased, and in the process must reveal the decision makers along the way. This particular question usually forces the prospect to reveal his or her true power within the decision-making process. With that understanding, the salesperson can move in the right direction.

WHY IS QUALIFYING SO IMPORTANT?

There are a number of reasons why qualifying is critically important to your call, not the least of which is saving time. Qualifying, when properly done, is far more powerful than most salespeople realize. It is because they have a limited view of qualifying that they fail to realize its power. Qualifying is key to making the right presentation. If you properly qualify the prospect's needs, you can focus your presentation on the things the prospect wants and values most. If you properly qualify objections, you will be able to better answer them and know that they will not return later in your selling effort. If you qualify tasks, you enable yourself to clearly determine the next step in the selling process.

Qualifying turns out to be the real backbone of any sales presentation. When the concepts of qualifying are applied properly, the sales process becomes easy and effortless. When the seller fails to qualify properly, he or she will constantly run into obstacles and delays. The seller will even find that there are numerous misunderstandings throughout the sales effort that make his or her work more difficult. This occurs because qualifying has the seller closing the sale step by step.

In every sale, controlling the call is the key. In the telephone sales call, the major component of control is the qualification. In a sense, qualifying is very similar to a trial close. When the prospect asks us to perform, if we qualify, we determine why this performance is necessary, what the performance will accomplish, what the result of the action will be, and, most important, based on the established criteria, what we can expect next. Understanding the correct next step in the sales process is extremely valuable. Qualifying often determines the next step for us, thus guiding us down the task list to the proper result.

THINGS THAT SHOULD BE QUALIFIED

In this next section I discuss those things that must be qualified and how specifically to accomplish that task.

Always Qualify Your Prospect and Company

Before making any kind of presentation, you must qualify both the company and the prospect. As I discussed in detail in the previous chapter, you must talk to the decision maker if you want the best chance to close a sale.

Typically, before you find the decision maker, you are talking to the organization. It is of course important to determine as early as possible if the company can potentially use your products or services. This can often be determined quite easily by questioning the reception and secretarial staff. Questions like *Do you use xyz products there at ABC Company?* will often generate the answers you need. Sometimes, however, depending on the complexity of the product or service you sell, you will need to reach a higher-level person, maybe even the decision maker, before qualification is possible.

Always Qualify the Decision Maker

Make sure you have a decision maker before making your presentation. One excellent way to qualify both the decision maker and the company is to ask about the decision process. We discussed this briefly in the previous chapter.

Your qualification of the decision maker should include the following:

- The decision maker's name
- The decision maker's title
- The authority of the decision maker in this decision
- The process by which the decision will be made

These are the key pieces of the decision maker's qualification. Obviously, you want to know the decision maker's name and title, but the authority and process are more important. By looking at one of these, you can often determine the major part of the other. It is the decision maker's authority that tells you how to present to him or her. It is the buying process that tells you what you need to do and who you need to convince to make the sale.

Key Qualification Questions You Might Ask the Decision Maker

1. How will your organization select the product you buy?
2. What is your specific role in the process?

3. Are there other individuals who will be a part of your decision who might need the information I'm giving you?
4. How will the person (or group) make the decision (whatever the decision might be)?
5. Are there other areas within the organization that might use our products or services that have different decision makers? (Or, do you make all the decisions for these types of products?)
6. What does a vendor have to do to get its product considered for purchase?

Each of these questions helps you to understand the process and level of authority of the decision maker as well as the other potential opportunities that might exist within the organization. The better your understanding of the process and who is really important, the better able you will be to develop the correct sales strategy.

Qualify Every Action Requested by the Prospect

Requests for actions by your prospect or customer should also be qualified. Qualifying a request is a great way to discover the motives for the request. Is the request really an objection, or is it the next step in the sales process?

By examining an action requested by the prospect, such as sending literature, it is possible to understand what the prospect will do with your action, and what is the next step in your sales process. For example, you might handle the literature request in the following way:

Request for literature:

Prospect: Could you please send me some information on your company?

Salesperson: Sure, I would be glad to send you some information. Just what is it you specifically were looking for?

64

Prospect: Well, I just wanted to read more about your company and its products.

Salesperson: Do you think, based on our discussion, that there is a possibility that you would be interested in our product line?

Prospect: Oh, yes. We are already using XYZ Company's widget, and I see you have those as well.

Salesperson: If I send you the information on our company and the widget, you should have that by Monday. How long will it take you to look at it?

Prospect: Why don't you give me a couple of days.

Salesperson: So would it be OK if I called you Wednesday?

Prospect: Sure, that would be fine.

Salesperson: OK, I will call you Wednesday. If everything is good, would you be willing to consider trying some samples at that point?

Prospect: Sure, if I like what you have, we can talk about getting a sample.

Salesperson: Great. I will call you Wednesday and we will see about getting you some samples.

This basic qualification of the literature request reveals that the prospect is serious about the product. It gives the salesperson the opportunity to find out where the prospect's real interest lies. Additionally, by closing the next step, the salesperson now knows what the objective of the next call will be and can prepare a presentation to close, in this case, the samples.

Always Qualify Objections and Answers to Questions

Many salespeople answer objections and other questions by the prospect without verifying (qualifying) the answers. This probably works more than 50 percent of the time, but often the answer given is not understood by or acceptable to the prospect. When this occurs, the question or objection often comes back later in the presentation.

The main part of qualifying questions and objections is to verify that the prospect understood the answer and that it is a valid answer in the prospect's mind—it is acceptable to the prospect. It is typical for the salesperson to tell the prospect, *That's no problem* and move on, assuming that the prospect accepts this answer, when in reality he or she does not. Often the prospect will not make an issue of this until later. By leaving this festering thought working in the prospect's mind, you may decrease the impact of the rest of your presentation because the prospect is preoccupied with the perceived problem.

Whenever a prospect gives you a question or an objection, after you give your answer, ask the prospect if he or she understands the answer you gave. Don't let the prospect off the hook; if you're not sure the prospect understands, take the time to explain the answer again, in more detail if necessary. Get a strong commitment from the prospect that the answer is a good one. Then, and especially with objections, ask the prospect if the answer solves the problem, or if the answer is acceptable. If the prospect doesn't agree with the solution, you have more work to do.

This methodology can save you a lot of time. Suppose, for example, you are selling a software package, and part of that package is a reporting tool. The prospect has some fairly complex reporting needs that require that data be sorted in some sophisticated ways; in other words, the program will need Boolean logic to accomplish the task. It just so happens that your program doesn't yet have a Boolean logic sort. In this case your product doesn't have what may be a critical feature. You will have to present the prospect with an alternative way to prepare the reports. If you simply tell the prospect, *It's not a big problem; you can just dump the data into a report writer and you will be fine,* the prospect may or may not agree. If you don't qualify the importance of the Boolean function and understand how it would be used, you don't know if your answer is acceptable. It may turn out that the Boolean function is really needed for only one report, and the company is always dumping its data into JKF Report Writer anyway. Thus your answer is fine. However, without a qualification, you don't know. If you give the presentation without qualifying, when you get to the end of your presentation, if you were wrong, you will spend a lot of time solving the problem and possibly rehashing other portions of your presentation because the prospect wasn't focused during your presentation. She was worried about your ability to create the proper reports.

Always Qualify the Next Step

As a salesperson, one of the most important things you can do to improve your results is to make sure you always qualify the next step. Whenever you hang up the phone (or leave the prospect's office), you should be clear about what is to happen next. You should know what the prospect is going to do, when he or she will do it, what the expected result is, and what the next step will be. In addition, you should make sure that the prospect knows what he or she is supposed to do, what you are going to do, and what the next step is.

When you leave a sales situation with the next step clearly planned, you will find that it is much easier to make progress on the next call. If the prospect was clear on the future course of events, he or she is more likely to hold up his or her end and complete the necessary tasks before you call. When the prospect doesn't complete them, you will have extra power in getting him or her to move promptly next time, as the prospect will feel bad about not doing what he or she said.

QUALIFYING MEANS CONTROLLING THE SALES PROCESS

Qualifying is much more involved than just asking the decision maker if he or she is responsible for buying your products or services. Qualifying involves making sure each piece of your presentation is solid as you put your sales story together. In the long run, qualifying makes the closing effort easier, because the buyer has agreed to all the pieces of the solution before you ask for the order. When I say qualify everything, what I am really saying is, understand what your prospect is thinking and why, understand what your prospect wants and how important it is to him or her. Only when this is accomplished can you hope to make a sale. By qualifying properly, you guarantee closure of each part of your sales process, and thus the final step when closing the order is easier.

What Have We Learned

- Qualifying is more than just asking if the company uses your product or if the person you're talking to is the decision maker.
- Qualifying questions are questions that educate the seller as to the selling environment.
- Failure to qualify leads to problems later in the sales cycle, usually because of bad assumptions.
- Don't just qualify the decision maker and the company, qualify all the transactions within your call, the next step, tasks you will do for the prospect, tasks the prospect will complete, and all questions and objections.
- Qualifying means control of the sales process.

Practice

Exercise 1. Take the following telephone call and analyze it for opportunities to qualify. Once you're done, go to the appendix at the end of the book and compare your analysis with ours. Write your answers on a separate piece of paper, using the line numbers to refer to where and what questions you would ask.

1. *Secretary:*		ABC Widget Corporation. This is Judy. How can I help you?
2. *Seller:*		Yes . . . I would like to reach the person in charge of purchasing marketing lists.
3. *Secretary:*		I'll transfer you to the marketing manager.
4. *Seller:*		Great!
5. *Buyer:*		Hello, this is Bob.
6. *Seller:*		Hi, Bob. My name is Rob Goodman with Superlists. How are you doing today?
7. *Buyer:*		Fine. What can I do for you?
8. *Seller:*		Well, as I said, Bob, I'm with Superlists and I just wanted to call and find out whether you folks buy marketing lists for your sales efforts.
9. *Buyer:*		Yes, we sure do.
10. *Seller:*		Just out of curiosity, Bob, what kinds of lists do you buy?

11. *Buyer:*		Well, we typically buy demographic lists of purchasers of gidits and fijits because we find those individuals are likely buyers of our products.
12. *Seller:*		Do you use the telephone or face-to-face selling for your widgets?
13. *Buyer:*		We actually use both. We have an inside sales team that qualifies and sells the lower-end accounts, and we have outside sales reps who follow up on those larger customers that need someone at their site to make the decision.
14. *Seller:*		So you would want lists that had the phone numbers as well as the address information, right?
15. *Buyer:*		Absolutely. Without the phone numbers, it takes too much work and time to find the prospect.
16. *Seller:*		Well, we are one of the best list compilation companies in the business and currently one of the top five companies from which you could buy your lists.

		We have very extensive lists for both gidit and fijit buyers, including some new international lists.
17.	*Buyer:*	That sounds good. Why don't you send me the information on your lists so I can take a look at it?
18.	*Seller:*	I'd be happy to; would you give me your address?
19.	*Buyer:*	Our address is . . . .
20.	*Seller:*	Great. I will send it out and give you a call back.
21.	*Buyer:*	Thanks. Bye.
22.	*Seller:*	Bye.

Exercise 2: Take one of your own sales calls and carefully analyze the places where you could have qualified better. You will find that most sales stories have logical places where qualification is needed. Find these key areas in your sales effort and develop key questions you should ask your prospects. You can use these questions in your presentation practice as well to improve your delivery of them.

[Sample answers to these exercises appear in the Appendix.]

Hints for Improving

1. Develop a set of questions that qualify your prospect and your prospect's company.

2. Develop a set of qualifying questions to discover the purchasing process for your product.
3. Develop a set of questions to qualify the major objections you get in your sales effort.
4. Practice using the questions in your presentation efforts.
5. After each presentation, think about the requests and questions your prospect posed and see if you qualified them properly. If you missed opportunities, pay attention in your next call to those specific issues if they arise again.
6. If you can't qualify, don't proceed with your presentation.

SEVEN

CALL OBJECTIVES AND THEIR IMPORTANCE

Conversations take on their own life. In a sales call, you are never quite sure where the prospect is going to take you. One minute you're talking business; the next, you might be discussing vacations. During the sales call, these extraneous casual conversations can be very dangerous. Often such conversations distract the salesperson from the purpose of the call. Casual conversations also take critical time from the call, often preventing the salesperson from completing the mission at hand. This is not to say that social conversation isn't necessary, just that as a salesperson you must be extremely careful with these distractions during a sales call.

TELEPHONE SALES CALLS HAVE TIME LIMITS

One of the most important things you can learn is that in a telephone sales call, there is a time limit. At some time, usually unknown, the prospect or customer is going to terminate the call. This means you must be effective and efficient in the delivery of your message. Without good call objectives, this can be difficult.

When you're sitting across from the prospect, the closure of the meeting is much more easily controlled by the salesperson than in a telephone conversation. Telephone conversations seem to have an exhaustion point where the prospect decides, "That is all we can do now—call me back or send me something." Understand the goals of your presentation and keep the conversation on track. Continually push the discussion forward in the direction of your call objectives or you will probably run out of time.

You must keep your presentation moving. One of the most frequent and critical errors salespeople make is failure to make progress during the call. Each sale has a set of tasks that must be completed before the sale can be made. This task list, which represents the call's objectives, or purpose, is the reason for the call in the first place. Whether the salesperson realizes it or not, every call must have a call objective. A prime example of the difficulties that occur when the call objectives are forgotten can be seen in the common difference between inbound and outbound calls. In working with salespeople, my experience has shown that those who receive calls have a much greater problem controlling the calls and making progress with the customer than those who are making proactive calls. This is because the inbound call recipient is distracted by the prospect's questions and forgets the objective of the conversation. Understanding call objectives solves this problem.

CASUAL CONVERSATIONS CAN BE DANGEROUS

Without call objectives, it is also possible to wander into areas where your opinions affect how the prospect feels about you. In some cases, your opinions might even affect the business relationship. There is an old saying that one should never discuss sex, politics, or religion with a customer, and this is probably good advice. One of the keys to becoming strong on the phone is learning to control these types of conversations and bring the prospect back to business. This is the real usefulness of call objectives.

Another critical factor is that the use of casual conversation often leads to casual presentation. As we have already discussed, you need to be constantly in your presentation voice if you wish to be effective. As we drift into personal conversations, we often move to our personal or casual voice. Then, as we move back to the presentation, we forget our presentation voice. This lessens the quality and effectiveness of our sales call.

WHAT IS A CALL OBJECTIVE?

A call objective is a goal for your call; it's what you want to accomplish. Obviously, you want to make a sale, and that is the overall objective. However, it is only one of the many objectives that occur within the call. You could call the final result of the call the primary objective. The primary objective then leads to the secondary objectives, which are, in fact, the tasks of the primary objective. For example, if you want to make a sale, you must first find the decision maker, the person who can make the purchase. This is only one of a number of steps (tasks) necessary to make the sale.

The objective of your call is really to accomplish all the tasks necessary to make the sale. Thus, if you make a list of the tasks required to close the customer, that list represents your call objectives. These tasks, or objectives, vary from sale to sale, although many of them are common. Here is a fairly generic list of tasks needed to make a sale:

1. Find the decision maker.
2. Qualify the prospect as the decision maker.
3. Qualify the company as a prospect.
4. Introduce the reason for your call.
5. Determine the potential of the prospect.
6. Tell your story. (Who are you? Why should the prospect do business with you?)
7. Develop the customer's needs.
8. Determine the proper solution and its value.
9. Close the customer on your offer.

This simple task list would probably fit into most sales processes, although the details might be different.

Call objectives are developed from tasks in the sales process. By having a list of objectives, you provide yourself with a map for your journey through the call. By sticking to the map as you make your presentation, you follow the logical course to your desired result. If you now take your task list and list below each task the questions that accomplish the task, you will have a sales presentation.

WHY ARE CALL OBJECTIVES IMPORTANT?

The importance of call objectives becomes much clearer if we just examine some average sales calls. We quickly realize that the salesperson is simply wandering through the call, often missing opportunities and forgetting critical steps in the sales process. We can see clearly how casual discussions lead the salesperson into a fog, where all direction of the call can be lost.

It turns out that for some reason, inbound calls are the most difficult for salespeople. In an inbound call, salespeople often mistake their objective for the sales call; they forget that the actual objective of the call is to sell, not just to service the caller. When customers call in, they usually start with a lot of questions. These questions often put the salesperson in what I call a *service mode,* and although it is possible to be aggressive in a service mode, it is not common. When barraged with questions, most salespeople simply answer them one after another. They forget that they need to do certain things in order to make the sale and relegate themselves to simply helping the customer with his or her questions. Unfortunately, if a salesperson is to be successful, these roles must be reversed. The salesperson must go directly after his or her objectives if he or she is going to be successful. The ironic thing is that salespeople love to have people call them because they feel it is a warmer lead. This is probably true, but based on my experience, most do better when they make the call. Let's look at a call I made to a computer dealer a couple of years ago.

The situation in this call is that I am interested in expanding my computer system so that I can perform better in my consulting practice. I want a better computer, and I don't have a printer. I made this call to begin my investigation of what I might be looking at to upgrade my system.

Before we examine the call, let's come up with a basic task list for a computer salesperson in a retail outlet handling a call.

Retail Outlet Sales Call Objectives

- Introduce yourself. Get to know the prospect (name, company, etc.).
- Find out the basic needs. Discover if you can help the prospect and what his or her specific needs are.
- Get the prospect to come to the store. In retail, if they don't come in, you're not going to make the sale.
- Close the prospect on a future call or appointment. If you cannot get the prospect into the store, you need to close some sort of a follow-up so that you get a second chance to bring the person to the store.

Computer Dealer—Inbound Call 1

> 1. **Buyer:** My name is Flyn. I'm interested in upgrading my computer system for my business. I am a consultant and I do a lot of desktop publishing—proposals, reports, seminars—that kind of thing—you know, book publishing type of things.
> 2. **Seller:** Are you printing to a laser printer?

This is the seller's first mistake. Notice that he is not following the objectives—he has not introduced himself and his company. You don't have relationships with people when you don't even know their names. This happens frequently with sellers who don't have clear objectives for their calls. They forget that they need to develop a relationship and start answering questions.

> 3. **Buyer:** Yes, but I don't have one yet. I am renting. It turns out that I am probably paying enough at the copy store to pay for the printer. I guess what I am really trying to decide is whether to go with an Apple II or an SE30.

Presenting a great opportunity—this guy needs a laser printer, maybe even more than a computer!

> 4. **Seller:** Well, if it was . . . well, you could go with a Mac IIcx.

The salesperson has now been given two major opportunities: the fact that I called about upgrading my system, and that I probably could use a laser printer. But notice how he is hooked on the suggested question, *Should I get an Apple II or an SE30?* This is called *service mode.* Rather than selling, the salesperson is trying to answer my questions. It's not that he should not answer my questions, but that he should do it in a way that answers his questions about the likelihood of my making a purchase. This call is made more difficult because the salesperson has not yet developed a relationship with me. I don't even know his name.

5. ***Buyer:*** Well, that's what I mean. The IIcx and the 30 are the same machine, right? Basically?

6. ***Seller:*** Basically the same microprocessors, but there are differences.

Read the sentence above, and even though you can't hear the voice, you can just tell that the salesperson is totally passive. This statement is not even a good explanation; it's as if the seller doesn't know what to say. He needs to be asking questions that will get the buyer interested in coming to the store. For example, *Mr. Buyer, have you seen these different machines? Do you know what the differences are? Maybe it would be valuable for you to come to the store and play with them a bit. Would you like to come in today and I'll show you the different possibilities?*

7. ***Buyer:*** The only differences that I know of are in the expansion.

8. ***Seller:*** Expansion, um, . . .

Now it is the buyer who is doing the explaining. The seller has completely lost control of the call and has no idea what to do. This is the result of not understanding his objectives. If he realized that he needs to bring this person into the store, he would be able to formulate the proper questions.

9. ***Buyer:*** And of course color is built into the IIcx.

10. ***Seller:*** Right. The 1.44 drive's the same, the 40-MB or 80-MB hard disk are all internal; that's equivalent to the SE30. The . . . I think on the SE30 the ROMs are removable too, just like they are on the IIcx.

11. ***Buyer:*** Yes.

12. ***Seller:*** So other than that, there's really not that much difference. They both have the same coprocessor.

13. ***Buyer:*** What would be the reason to go to the II rather than the 30? I mean, there is a lot of money involved.

14. ***Seller:*** Right.

Here again the seller is lost; he is not even answering the buyer's question. The seller should explain the differences, mostly expansion, and then use this to invite the buyer to the store. For example, *Mr. Buyer, the major difference between the systems is that the IIcx is quite a bit more flexible with regard to expansion and you can have color. Have you seen the IIcx? Why don't we set up a time for you to come by and I'll show you both systems side by side?*

15. **Buyer:** What kind of expansion would you have to be looking at where the II would be useful versus the SE30, or what would the differences be? That's what I am trying to figure out. The big question is, do I want to spend the extra money and have that extra expansion available and have the color available, or am I just not going to use that stuff in the future, so it would be a waste of money? There is not a whole lot of stuff to do in color. . . . I have the Persuasion program, and that program has facilities for color.

16. **Seller:** Um.

17. **Buyer:** And so that's one area where I might use the color, but you know, as far as . . . you know, if I am going to pay 2,000 extra dollars, am I going to get my money's worth doing that? I don't think so. So do you have some ideas there as far as the abilities of the machine . . .

18. **Seller:** Well, if you don't need the expansion or the color . . .

19. **Buyer:** I guess my biggest question is . . . I can get along without the color, I think.

20. **Seller:** If you can, then the SE30 is the one you want to look at.

21. **Buyer:** I guess my concern is on the expansion, but I really don't know what you would expand into. What normally are people doing with the extra slots?

22. **Seller:** Um . . . accelerator cards, DOS coprocessor cards, um . . . internal modems . . .

23. *Buyer:* OK, as far as plugging things into the back of the machine, let's say you wanted to have, say, both a laser and a dot matrix printer plugged in and have a modem as well. The SE30 would handle all that with no problem, wouldn't it?
24. *Buyer:* Um . . .
25. *Buyer:* Even my Mac will handle two printers.
26. *Seller:* But it won't handle two printers and a modem, and neither will the SE30.
27. *Buyer:* OK.
28. *Seller:* The modem has got to be in one of those ports.
29. *Buyer:* OK, if you were really serious about that configuration, then . . .
30. *Seller:* You would get a switch box.
31. *Buyer:* Could you use the expansion slot for one of those?
32. *Seller:* No, not at all. I don't even think there are that many internal modems made for the Macintosh.
33. *Buyer:* So with either machine you're going to be in the same boat if you want to run two printers.
34. *Seller:* Right.
35. *Buyer:* If you run a laser printer, then the phone port is still free for the modem, right?
36. *Seller:* Right.
37. *Buyer:* Because it uses the printer port when you use a laser.
38. *Seller:* Correct.

During the past eight or so exchanges, the buyer has been doing all the selling; the seller is just along for the ride. Now the problem that plagues all telephone sales calls occurs: The buyer has the information he wanted and he is ready to hang up. Look at the next statement by the buyer. You can tell by the tone that this call is about to come to an end. The buyer is now looking at price.

39. *Buyer:* Well, that's a little bit of information. What kind of money do you spend to get an SE30? I

      would probably get it with 4 MB memory and at least an 80-MB hard drive. Is there a package where I get the memory and save some money?

40. *Seller:* It's cheaper to get the 4 MB with the 80.
41. *Buyer:* So they have a setup with 4 MB and an 80 that saves you money?
42. *Seller:* Yes.
43. *Buyer:* OK. Well, you have been pretty helpful, and I have some basic literature on the thing . . . what I probably should do is just come down and take a look at it.

The perfect invitation to the seller.

44. *Seller:* Yes, we have it on display.
45. *Buyer:* OK, thank you very much.

Oops! What happened? The seller, again not aware of the real objectives of his call, loses his way and forgets to close. Not only that, he never gets the critical information from the buyer that would allow a follow-up call. He doesn't even know the buyer's name, or if he does, he's never used it once! How can you develop a good relationship without knowing someone's name? You can't.

46. *Seller:* Bye-bye.
47. *Buyer:* Good-bye.

Call Summary

This call offered a multitude of opportunities for the seller. He had a real prospect and a couple of major opportunities to pursue. Unfortunately, the seller missed because he didn't know what he should be accomplishing in the call. There were other mistakes as well, but you can see by comparing the list of objectives with the call that the seller really didn't understand the situation.

82

END OF CALL

It is very instructive to analyze calls in this way. You can do this yourself by simply recording your calls, transcribing them, and reviewing them.

Let's look at a different call now. This one comes from a salesperson in the staffing industry. The call objectives here might be as follows:

1. Find one of the many decision makers. They would typically provide staffing for a number of different departments and managers.
2. Qualify the prospect and the company.
3. Determine the opportunities with the decision maker.
4. Develop the requirements and needs of the decision maker.
5. Close the sale.
6. If there is no opportunity, look for other decision makers.

Staffing Company Sales Call

In this call, the caller is already aware of the company and the HR manager's name from a previous attempt to reach him. Additionally, he has indirect information about an opportunity in the technical support group for some temporary personnel and the fact that the HR manager handles these issues.

1. *Secretary:*	This is AVI. May I help you?
2. *Salesperson:*	Yes, I want to talk to Tod in human resources, but first can I get the spelling of his last name, please?
3. *Secretary:*	Sure. It's Hickman, that's H-I-C-K-M-A-N.

This is good, using the receptionist to gather a bit more information.

4. *Salesperson:*	Great! Is he in, please?
5. *Secretary:*	I'll ring, thank you.
6. *Salesperson:*	Thank you.

7. *Prospect:*	Tod Hickman.
8. *Salesperson:*	Tod, this is Bob Salesman calling from ABC Staffing. How are you doing?
9. *Tod:*	OK.
10. *Salesperson:*	Good. We're a technical contracting service, and we specialize in MIS placements, and I was just a little curious about what type of contractor usage you have at AVI, and if your . . .

It's too early for this statement (line 10); the prospect hasn't been qualified. For example, it would be better to say, *I understand you are the manager of human resources; is that correct?* followed by *One of my associates became aware that your technical support manager may be looking for some people; is that correct? And if I understand correctly, in the past you have hired contractors, then once they proved themselves, you moved them to permanent positions. . . . Is it possible I might assist you in filling these positions?*

As in our previous call, the seller is not clearly aware of the objectives of his call; he forgot to qualify the prospect.

11. *Tod:*	We're trying to phase out all the contractors to the greatest extent possible. We're in a very, very rapid growth mode; I've hired eighty-five people in the last ten months, and a . . .

Now the prospect gives an objection. This may be real, or it may be a response to the seller's failure to develop a relationship: "Go away; I'm OK without any more help; I don't know you."

The seller in this case has also failed to make the connection to his knowledge of the situation. If he referred to the specific opportunities that he is aware of, he would have a "warmer" call. Bringing up the fact that he is aware of the positions and previous methods of hiring gives him a better chance.

12. *Salesperson:*	My goodness . . .

Another chance to use your referral: *What about the tech support positions? I understand you're currently looking, and in the past you have used contractors.* This question would have again brought the seller into a better position.

13.	**Tod:**	. . . and we need 'em periodically, but for the most part we have probably five in our whole company . . .
14.	**Salesperson:**	I see.
15.	**Tod:**	. . . so we're not looking to put on any contractors.

Here the salesperson is into the presentation but has not yet developed any relationship with the prospect. Tod doesn't even know the seller's company or why he should consider it in the future. At this point, the salesperson is just another name. Additionally, Tod has stated his objections and the seller has not addressed them.

Looking at the objectives list, we see that the seller has passed over the qualification and failed to develop the needs he was aware of when he started the call. Now, because he doesn't have a relationship developed, he is getting objections.

16.	**Salesperson:**	I see. Do you think it would be OK if I sent some information just for backup, in case you run into some problems?

Now, without even a good relationship developed, this statement begs to get off the phone. Where is a closing question? Where is an answer to the prospect's objections? What did he get from the call? The seller should try to address the objection and then try the referral approach, mentioning the positions he was aware of when he started the call and trying to close a commitment from Tod on the next contractor he needs!

17.	**Tod:**	That's fine.
18.	**Salesperson:**	OK, good. Are you still at 123 Ban Street?
19.	**Tod:**	Right.

20. **Salesperson:** OK, good enough. And your exact title is manager of human resources?

This question belongs in the beginning of the call, not as an afterthought. This is a qualification question—it's almost pointless here.

21. **Tod:** Director of human services.
22. **Salesperson:** Director of . . . I'm glad I asked. OK, typically what type of contractors do you use when you need them?

Finally, the salesperson starts to develop the prospect's needs. Up to this point the salesperson hasn't asked any of the key questions. Because he is not aware of what he should be doing, he wandered through the call and was put into a daze by the prospect's objection.

23. **Tod:** Um, systems administrators, um, could be DBAs but primarily systems administrators.
24. **Salesperson:** Right, OK, well, that is right along our lines.
25. **Tod:** Unix background, that kind of stuff.
26. **Salesperson:** Exactly. Well, that's what we specialize in.
27. **Tod:** Um.
28. **Salesperson:** What department is usually the one who uses those?
29. **Tod:** Um . . . MIS . . . the MIS department.
30. **Salesperson:** And when you do use contractors, it would be coordinated by you?
31. **Tod:** Yes.

In the last five or six statements the seller got Tod talking about potential needs again. He even began to tell Tod how he could help—where is the knockout punch?

32. **Salesperson:** OK, good enough. Let me get this information off to you, and then I'll follow up to make sure it got there.

We've been hit, we've been hit, pull the ejection handle, bail out, bail out! Although the door was reopened, the salesperson already has his mind set on a failure and doesn't seize the opportunity.

33. **Tod:** Thank you.
34. **Salesperson:** Thanks for your time, Tod.
35. **Tod:** Bye.
36. **Salesperson:** Bye-bye.

Summary

This was a great-looking prospect going in—at least, he was warm to start. However, the salesperson failed to go for what was on the table, and to use the information he had to work with in the beginning.

End of Call

You can see from our two real-life calls how easy it is to go through the call and get nothing. In both cases the prospects were interested and viable, and in both cases the salesperson missed the objectives of the call and failed to even be in a position to make any offer.

How Do You Set Call Objectives?

By now it should be very obvious that call objectives are very important to your success. Even the simplistic list of objectives we developed for each call would have substantially helped the seller if he had followed them. The question now arises, how do you set good call objectives?

The First Rule of Call Objectives: The Best Call Objectives Are Flexible

It is obvious that the primary objective of the call is to make the sale or, in a telemarketing environment, to make the appointment or get the prospect interested in our product or service. Making the sale on the first call is not always practical, and in most sales there are a number of key tasks that must be accomplished before closure can be made. If our only objective is making the sale, this is not very helpful in guiding our presentation effort. We need more detail. Each call may proceed differently and thus require us to move from one objective to another. It may be a sale where there are more objectives than can be accomplished in one call; thus the list of objectives to complete changes from call to call.

Another reason you must be flexible is that prospects may show different needs from those you originally determined. You may call a prospect who ultimately disqualifies himself or herself as a buyer or decision maker, which changes your objective back to finding the decision maker.

The Second Rule of Call Objectives: You Must Understand the Steps in Your Sales Process

The only way to develop a good set of objectives is to clearly understand your sales process. You must know what it takes to make the sale. What must happen before you can actually sell someone? Selling is very much like building a car: If you don't know what parts you need, you won't know the order of assembly, or how to proceed with building the car. Without knowledge of the sales process, confusion will reign, as we saw in the two sales call examples above.

Breaking Objectives Into Tasks

By examining the sales process, we can break it into its primary parts. As an example, let's take a retail stereo salesperson. This individual's job is to sell audio equipment. When someone calls, it is quite evident that a sale is not going to be made on the telephone. In this situation, we must determine what needs to happen on the telephone if we are to make the sale. Well, quite obviously, we must get the prospect into the store. If the prospect won't come to the store, she or he probably won't buy! This becomes our primary objective for the telephone call: to get the prospect into the store. We must now break this objective into tasks, as follows:

Phone Calls Tasks (Objectives)

1. *Find out who the prospect is.* The only way you have a chance of working with the prospect is to know him or her. You must find out the prospect's name and telephone number (so that you can follow up if necessary). Without a name it is very hard to develop a relationship.

2. *Introduce yourself.* Once again, without letting the prospect know who you are, it will be very difficult to establish any relationship. This is a frequent mistake of salespeople: The prospect calls and starts asking questions, and the salesperson never even bothers to find out who he or she is talking to or to introduce him- or herself and the organization. Without such an exchange of information, it is almost impossible to create a relationship.

3. *State the reason for your call.* In the act of proactive calling, people are as uncomfortable talking to someone when they don't know the reason for the call as they are talking with an unknown caller. You must tell people early on why you are calling if you want them to relax enough to develop a rapport. Similarly, when you get a call, you should tell the prospect what you can do for her or him, and how you will do it.

4. *Give the company story.* It is nice to introduce yourself, but it is also important to introduce your company. Many prospects call companies they are not familiar with. Like talking to someone whose name you don't know, talking to an organization you are not familiar with makes you uncomfortable. As a salesperson you must introduce your company if you want to develop a prospect who is confident in your overall ability to furnish a solution. In many cases the prospect may be familiar with your organization in a negative way, and you would surely want to

know that up front in any sales situation. You always want to give the prospect a pat on the back for calling (if he or she called) and tell the prospect why he or she is talking to the right organization for this particular product or service. Neither of the salespeople above said one word about their organizations, not a single word. How are prospects supposed to remember how good you are if you don't tell them?

5. *Qualify the prospect.* Now that the prospect is comfortable, the introduction having developed a rapport, you can begin to question the prospect about his or her potential. Asking these questions earlier will usually put the prospect off, make him or her defensive, and thus thwart your efforts in making a presentation. In our example, the qualification would be to find out first what the buyer is looking for, whether you carry such items, whether you can furnish a solution, and whether the buyer is ready to make a purchase. If any of these is not true, you're not going to make the sale.

6. *Make the sale!* Now you need to make the sale! No, not sell the prospect what he or she is looking for, sell him or her on coming to the store! Remember, that was the goal of the call. It makes no difference whether the prospect called you or you made a prospecting call, the only reasonable goal is to bring the prospect to the store where he or she can buy. Doing this requires you to give the prospect a reason for coming. It might be to see the variety of items you have, to compare the quality of the different brands, to look at some other options not yet considered, or whatever—that is your only objective. Giving the prospect other information about the desired purchase is dangerous; it educates the prospect for the next salesperson. Get the prospect in the store first; then if you give him or her an education, you at least have the chance of making the sale.

What I have done here is taken the major factors of the call objective and defined each. By simply thinking about the telephone call based on the primary objective (bring the prospect to the store), we discovered six key things that need to be done, the last being the ultimate objective for the call.

Every sales call can be broken down in the same way. Of

course, the more knowledge of selling you have to start with, the better your objectives list will be. However, even if you are not so experienced, as you deliver your presentation, you will see things that are necessary to your list that you missed at first.

With this process, any salesperson answering the phone could deliver a good presentation just by using the list. Make this simple effort for each of the different types of sales calls you make. Creating an objectives list and using it to guide your calls will improve the quality of your telephone sales efforts.

The Third Rule of Call Objectives: Objectives Are Always Pieces of Your Final Sales Goal

Remember that the objectives are made of the tasks in the sale, the tasks being that information needed for the prospect to make the buying decision.

Using Sales Tasks to Guide Your Call

Using the tasks to guide your call is a simple way to create effective sales presentations. Once you understand what the correct tasks are and their proper order, you have a presentation. The further you break them down, the more detail you will get. For example, one of the audio salesperson's tasks is the task of finding out about the prospect. This task could be further developed by listing the specific information that we would like to have:

1. Name
2. Address
3. Telephone number
4. Product interest
5. Budget
6. Time frame for purchase
7. Preferred brands

You will find that every task in your sales call can be broken up into smaller tasks. At some point, as in the above list, the further breakdown is the question to be asked. List these questions and you will have as your end result a detailed presentation.

If you keep track of completed and uncompleted tasks for each prospect, you know exactly what to do on the next call. The order of the tasks tells you what you need to do next in any situation. If you're using some sort of contact management system or have a folder on the prospect, you can keep track of which tasks are complete and which need to be completed. This will allow you to plan your next call. If you know what is missing to make the sale, it becomes easier to make progress. You don't end up rehashing your first call; instead, you ask the key questions necessary to complete the task list and thus make the sale.

Make Progress in Every Call

To make progress is all we can ask of ourselves. As we discussed in detail earlier, attitude is the key to success. If you don't feel like a winner, you won't act and sound like one. With the task list you can see if you are making progress. Because of the task list, it is now very easy to make progress, as you clearly know what to do and when to do it.

Focus on the tasks that lead to the objective you have set for your call, complete one, then move on to the next. Eventually, you will complete all the tasks and the sale will be yours. Patience is the key to progress; if you keep chipping away at the tasks, you will eventually reach the objective. Each objective creates a new set of objectives to fulfill and a new task list.

What Have We Learned?

- Telephone sales calls have unknown time limits; you must keep moving.
- Casual conversation can lead to problems.
- Call objectives are the tasks of the sales process.
- Every call should have specific call objectives.
- Set clear, flexible call objectives.

Practice

1. Look at the plan that was developed in the Chapter 5 Appendix section (under Practice Exercise 1) for a manufacturing call, and use that plan to analyze your own call.
2. Take your own sales call and list the objectives you should be pursuing in your calls.
3. Give the primary reasons that call objectives are important.
4. What is a call objective?

[Sample answers to these exercises appears in the Appendix.]

Hints for Improving

1. Examine your sales process for the key tasks that must be completed to make the sale.
2. Develop a set of questions that accomplishes each task.
3. Make sure you understand the flow of the sales process. Some things can be done out of order, whereas others must follow a specific time line.
4. Until you have mastered the process, use a checklist to assist you during your calls.

EIGHT

PERSISTENT CURIOSITY AND INVESTIGATION

LEAVE NO STONE UNTURNED!

As salespeople we must be highly attuned to our prospects' words, and not only to what they say, but to what they imply— and especially to what they *don't* say. In this respect, I was very lucky in selling. In selling, being insatiably curious, as I am, is a tremendous advantage. The advantage of this hunger for information is that it leads you to opportunities—not only opportunities for more sales, but opportunities to close those more difficult prospects. Many times we have trouble closing the sale simply because we can't find the prospect's real need or objection. Prospects aren't always that clear themselves on what it is that makes them wary of their purchase. Sometimes they just feel uncomfortable and can't tell you exactly why. You probably can remember the same feelings yourself if you think about past purchases. You will often hear the excuse, "I need to think about it." This objection is a sure sign that the real objections are still buried somewhere in the prospect's head. Curiosity will often help you to track down those elusive objections in indirect ways you might not think of, giving you additional chances to close the sale.

Your goal is to find all the reasons your prospect would buy. The more reasons you find, the more reasons you can present as benefits when you close the sale. Prospects make many statements throughout the course of a sales presentation that give clues to what is going on, or to opportunities that exist. I call these opportunities "doors." A "door" is a statement by the prospect that in one way or another affects your ability to close the sale. Yes, this sounds like a fairly general statement, but it's those general, innocent-sounding statements that lead to opportunities when investigated. Let's take a look at one of the previous telephone calls and see some examples of these "door" statements.

Computer Store—Inbound Call

    3. *Buyer:* Yes, but I don't have one yet. I am renting. It turns out that I am probably paying enough at the copy store to pay for the printer. I guess

> what I am really trying to decide is whether to
> go with an Apple II or an SE30.

This statement by the buyer, in response to the question *Do you have a laser printer?* represents a giant opportunity. In the actual call, the salesperson never even responded to the printer opportunity, and the call ended without any significant result. This statement offers the chance to make a whole new presentation. Whether or not the buyer can make up his mind on the computer upgrade, this statement indicates that his mind is almost made up as to the value of having a printer. It must be investigated.

> **43. *Buyer:*** OK. Well, you have been pretty helpful, and I have some basic literature on the thing . . . what I probably should do is just come down and take a look at it.

This statement also opens a big door. The goal of the call, as we discovered, should probably be to get the buyer to the store. Here the buyer offers that as a solution. The seller must respond and investigate the possibilities for getting the buyer to do just that: come to the store.

These two statements both represent doors, one being a sales opportunity and the other being a buying statement. You can see how easily the salesperson passed them over during the conversation. However, the most useful statements are often the ones that don't say something important. These, of course, are also the most difficult for salespeople to spot. Let's look at some examples:

"I can help you": This statement is often in response to the question *Are you the decision maker?* If you are curious, you ask yourself, *How?* and *Who are you?* Many salespeople don't recognize this gatekeeper trap and go on with their presentations.

"I'm responsible for purchasing widgets for this division": Most salespeople would react to this statement (door) with their presentation, obviously having the decision maker in hand. However, this statement covers a number of opportunities—and potential pitfalls if not properly investigated. First and foremost, *Who makes the decisions for the other divisions? (and what other divisions are there?)*. This represents a real opportunity to open other opportunities. If it turns out that this prospect doesn't need your service or product, a referral to other entities within the company is definitely indicated. Obviously, once you make the sale to this prospect, the same external opportunities may exist. All of this should be investigated sooner or later. This statement also raises the question, *Do these divisions have some interconnected relationship relative to the decision to buy?* In other words, will you get to the end of your presentation and discover that your prospect needs to submit this offer to the other divisions and get a unanimous approval before the purchase is made?

"I know about your company": This is another of those statements that salespeople impale themselves on because they don't investigate what the prospect means. If the prospect had a bad experience or was told a horror story about your company by someone else, and you don't investigate what happened, you may find yourself on your knees after your closing question. When the prospect comes back with *Last time I did business with you guys, it cost me . . .* in response to your closing question, it is very difficult to solve the problem and make a sale.

Besides such statements, it is always necessary to investigate objections. Don't take any objection at face value. People have a tendency to make up reasons when they are fearful of buying. Additionally, as mentioned before, sometimes people really don't know why they are concerned about making the final decision. If you don't investigate objections, you will often miss opportunities.

THE KEY TO CURIOSITY

If you are not a curious person by nature, if the prospect's statements don't leap out at you begging more questions and investigations, then fully understanding the tasks necessary to complete the sale is your final goal. Understanding the sales tasks will allow you to use a more mechanical method to discover opportunities. Using the tasks as a baseline, you can apply prospect statements to each of the tasks, looking for a conflict or effect that may exist between what is said and your goal of closing the prospect.

Let's take one of our previously developed sales task lists to demonstrate how you can mechanically solve the curiosity problem.

Retail Outlet Sales Call Objectives

▪ Find the decision maker. (Because our objective list was created for an inbound call, I have added this objective to make it viable for a proactive effort.)

▪ Introduce yourself. Get to know the prospect (name, company, etc.).

▪ Find out the basic needs. Discover if you can help the prospect and specifically what the needs are.

▪ Get the prospect to come to the store. In retail, if they don't come in, you're not going to make the sale.

▪ Close the prospect on a future call or appointment. If you cannot get the prospect into the store, you need to close some sort of a follow-up so that you get a second chance to bring the person to the store.

If you don't come up with the questions naturally, you can simply compare each of the prospect's statements to the task list. When comparing, look for a potential conflict between your objective and what the prospect has said. Let's take the statements we just examined and compare them to this list. Assume for the moment that you are a salesperson in a retail computer store (or selling any type of appliance). The above objectives list fits any product of this type, as it is always true that the prospect will have to come to the store to buy, and it is very unlikely that he or she will buy on the telephone. In this example you are calling on businesses to sell computer systems.

Situation 1

You have just called and asked for the person who is responsible for the purchase of computer equipment. The secretary says,

That would be Bob Jones. I'll transfer you. Bob Jones comes on the phone and you say, *I was looking for the person who purchases the computers for your business.* Bob says, *I can help you.*

You must now compare your situation to the task list. You are looking for any indication that this statement, *I can help you,* might prevent you from reaching your objective: bringing the prospect into the store. In this case, the list doesn't directly give you the clue you need. However, it should be obvious that the only person you really want an appointment with is the person who does the buying. Thus, you must evaluate whether what Bob has said so far is enough to let you be sure he is the real decision maker. Do Bob's answers confirm the fact that he is the buyer? Even though the secretary told you that he is the right person, and you asked him the question, your question was not direct enough for you to be completely assured that you have the right person. At this point you should ask one more qualifying question to make sure Bob is not one of the decision maker's gofers and just trying to handle the call.

Situation 2

If Bob convinces you that he is the decision maker and buyer, you can proceed to introduce yourself and your store. At this point Bob says, *I know you guys.*

If you take that statement and compare it to your task of getting Bob to the store, you realize that should Bob know something bad about your company, he probably won't come in. This makes it necessary for you to ask questions about Bob's experience or knowledge of your company.

You are simply looking for ways in which the statement made by the prospect affects your ability to achieve your objectives. The prospect's statement may affect one or all of your objectives. For this reason it is critically important that you know and understand your objectives completely. During the call you will have to make this decision quickly as the prospect talks.

Let's look at another situation and see how it works.

Situation 3

Let's assume that during your conversation with Bob, he indicates a real interest in some purchases. Within that conversation, he says, *Joan in the programming group just got a bunch of machines just like these. I'm really looking forward to getting our group upgraded to 586s.*

This relatively innocent statement escapes most salespeople, and they simply skip over it and proceed with their presentation. After all, the prospect just confirmed how interested and close to buying he is—keep selling, right? Wrong. This statement reveals a number of dangers. Before reading on, see what kind of a list you can come up with.

Bob has placed a potentially major land mine in the way of your sale. Here is why: What if, after you convince Bob to come visit you, he talks to Joan about his purchase? Will she recommend that he come to your store, or will she possibly send Bob to the store she bought from? Will he ask Joan about the service provided by her vendor before coming to see you? Furthermore, if he buys the computers, how come it was Joan and not he who purchases those units? Is Bob the real decision maker, or just one decision maker? You might even want to know whether Joan was happy with the computers she received. These are all questions that arise from Bob's statement of interest in getting his computers.

Looking at the objectives list, this statement could affect whether Bob will come to the store or not. Bob's statement may lead to questions about his ability to make decisions, whether there are others with decision-making authority, and how the vendor may be chosen.

Curiosity is almost impossible to teach. If it isn't natural, you need to clearly see the relationship between what someone says and your goals. You need to find the ways in which statements indicate a possible effect on the goals of your call, as we did in the examples above. You can go through your presentation mentally and look for statements you have heard or think of that have these potential obstacles to your close, and then prepare the questions that discover the facts.

SEEKING IMAGINED OPPORTUNITIES

Using the prospect's statements as a reference, you need to be thinking all the time about opportunities that might exist in the background. Look at every statement with the question, "Is there a potential for more business in what is being said?" Every statement by the prospect should be generating more questions than it answers. This is why asking lots of questions about the company, its needs, and the decision process during the needs development stage of your call is so critically important.

Remember that, as the seller, you will see far more usefulness for your product or service than the prospect does. You will better understand how the prospect could utilize the power of your product's features and advantages. To take advantage of your knowledge, you must have a clear understanding of the prospect's environment and how the product will be used. Prospects may not always completely understand your product or service. They may come to you for a product with only a partial knowledge of your product's usefulness. Thus, you have the opportunity to expand the reasons the prospect might buy. Once your understanding of the prospect's potential is complete, you will have the opportunity to offer the prospect a number of solutions.

An Example

Say you are selling computers. The prospect comes to you because she wants to get a computer for her business. She tells you that she will be using it to do word processing and to take care of her accounting. Her business is the distribution of widgets. If you were to ask some questions, you would find out a number of things that could increase your chances of making a sale by increasing the number of benefits you could provide. For example, she has a sales force that currently calls on customers by phone, using a manual system to track their accounts. This piece of information tells you that the prospect may benefit from a contact management system. Asking further questions, you may find out that she also has an inventory system that is currently kept manually. This would allow you to present the prospect with the idea of automating that system and letting the computer keep control of inventory levels. In addition, you might discover that the prospect is writing orders by hand; this phase of her business might also be computerized to her advantage if it can be tied to the inventory system.

So you started with a prospect who was serious about a computer for only two reasons, word processing and accounting. Now with a few questions you have found four or five other significant benefits from buying the computer. This not only increases the size of your sale, but increases the reasons the prospect should spend her money.

This example will work for almost any product. As we stated, you will always see more benefits than the prospect, but you have to carefully investigate what the prospect says and how he or she intends to use the product in order to find the additional benefits.

Don't Leave "Potholes" in Your Sales Highway

One of the main reasons you must be careful in your investigation is that you don't want to leave problems that will come up when you try to close. Selling is like a trip on the highway. When you go to close the prospect, you're traveling that highway at the maximum speed. If you have left a problem, it is like a pothole in your highway. The bump may just knock your alignment out, or it may give you a flat tire. In either case, it affects your ability to get the sale.

Your sale is also very much like a trip across the country. You need to have a map if you are to successfully find your way. In selling, this map is your call objectives and sales tasks. If you skip a turnoff, you miss your destination, just as if you miss a key task, you will fail to close because all is not in order for the prospect to make the decision.

You need to build sales roads that don't have "potholes" so that you don't wreck your close (car) in the most important part of the journey. In a telephone presentation, you must not leave any issues unresolved. On the telephone, even if you cover everything that comes up in the presentation to the prospect, there may be problems. This occurs because on the telephone we are blind; we can't always see everything that is happening. If you are not very aware of the potential problems, and you don't take time to ask all the proper questions, you may find yourself in a

103

jam in the final hour. That is why you must construct a carefully thought-out task list and stick to it, completing each and every step before trying to get the order.

What Have We Learned?

- We must be curious and investigative if we want to discover opportunities.
- We must examine customer statements for opportunities that were not directly mentioned.
- We must consistently compare our objectives and tasks to the prospect's statements to determine if these statements will affect our ability to succeed.
- Prospects and customers don't always have a clear idea of what they really want or need, because they don't always fully understand the product they are buying.

Practice

Take this previously analyzed call and note where you think further investigation might be valuable. See our analysis in the appendix.

1. *Secretary:*		This is AVI. May I help you?
2. *Salesperson:*		Yes, I want to talk to Tod in human resources, but first can I get the spelling of his last name, please?
3. *Secretary:*		Sure. It's Hickman, that's H-I-C-K-M-A-N.
4. *Salesperson:*		Great! Is he in, please?
5. *Secretary:*		I'll ring, thank you.
6. *Salesperson:*		Thank you.
7. *Prospect:*		Tod Hickman.
8. *Salesperson:*		Tod, this is Bob Salesman calling from ABC Staffing. How are you doing?
9. *Tod:*		OK.
10. *Salesperson:*		Good. We're a technical contracting service, and we specialize in MIS placements, and I was just a little curious about what type of contractor usage you have at AVI, and if your . . .
11. *Tod:*		We're trying to

		phase out all the contractors to the greatest extent possible. We're in a very, very rapid growth mode; I've hired eighty-five people in the last ten months, and a . . .
12.	*Salesperson:*	My goodness . . .
13.	*Tod:*	. . . and we need 'em periodically, but for the most part we have probably five in our whole company . . .
14.	*Salesperson:*	I see.
15.	*Tod:*	. . . so we're not looking to put on any contractors.
16.	*Salesperson:*	I see. Do you think it would be OK if I sent some information just for backup, in case you run into some problems?
17.	*Tod:*	That's fine.
18.	*Salesperson:*	OK, good. Are you still at 123 Ban Street?
19.	*Tod:*	Right.
20.	*Salesperson:*	OK, good enough. And your exact title is manager of human resources?
21.	*Tod:*	Director of human services.
22.	*Salesperson:*	Director of . . . I'm glad I asked. OK,

		typically what type of contractors do you use when you need them?
23.	*Tod:*	Um, systems administrators, um, could be DBAs but primarily systems administrators.
24.	*Salesperson:*	Right, OK, well, that is right along our lines.
25.	*Tod:*	Unix background, that kind of stuff.
26.	*Salesperson:*	Exactly. Well, that's what we specialize in.
27.	*Tod:*	Um.
28.	*Salesperson:*	What department is usually the one who uses those?
29.	*Tod:*	Um . . . MIS . . . the MIS department.
30.	*Salesperson:*	And when you do use contractors, it would be coordinated by you?
31.	*Tod:*	Yes.
32.	*Salesperson:*	OK, good enough. Let me get this information off to you, and then I'll follow up to make sure it got there.
33.	*Tod:*	Thank you.
34.	*Salesperson:*	Thanks for your time, Tod.
35.	*Tod:*	Bye.
36.	*Salesperson:*	Bye-bye.

[*An analysis of this exercise appears in the Appendix.*]

Hints for Improving

1. Develop a complete and detailed task list for your sales call.
2. Develop question lists for each task, making sure you cover all the information you need to complete the task.
3. Pay attention to the objections you get in your calls—they usually represent unanswered questions in your presentation.
4. Make a list of key objections and answers so that you are ready to handle them efficiently when they come up.
5. Study the objections to find the reasons they might occur. This knowledge will allow you to prepare questions for your presentation that will let you avoid them in the first place.

NINE

CLOSING

Probably the most important part of every call is the seller's use of closing skills and techniques. It is absolutely critical to you as a seller that you close relentlessly throughout the presentation. You always want to remember the old cliché "Follow the ABCs of closing!"—ABCs being an acronym for *always be closing*. Prospects very rarely just buy. In most cases you have to ask for the order if you expect to be successful. As a salesperson, you cannot afford to be afraid to ask the tough questions. Many salespeople, rather than asking directly for the order, will make a closing statement like, *Well, Ms. Prospect, what do you think?* Of course the prospect promptly answers, to the dismay of the salesperson, *That's a good idea; I will think about it.* After all, this is a logical answer; you asked the prospect what she thought.

The primary reason this happens, besides the fear of closing that is present in all of us, is that the salesperson has not done enough of the groundwork to make a proper close. This makes the real closing question almost seem inappropriate, as indeed it is. Without completely developing the customer's needs, it is very difficult to make a reasonable offer.

However, there is more to closing than just asking for the order at the end of your presentation, as the cliché *always be closing* suggests. Thus, our first rule of closing is this cliché.

THE FIRST RULE OF CLOSING: ALWAYS BE CLOSING

Closing the sale starts during the opening of the call and continues throughout the entire sales call. This is more critical to the success of the sale on the telephone than in a face-to-face transaction. The difference is the ability to see the objections more clearly when dealing with someone face to face. In the telephone call, closing is the main vehicle for discovering the prospect's motives and needs.

The proper use of closing is to close consistently throughout your presentation on all types of issues and transactions, not just the question of buying. Many salespeople are unaware of these opportunities to preclose the sale using different closing techniques.

Our ultimate goal is to close each little piece of the sale as we make our presentation. In doing this, we get to the conclusion of the presentation with only a very small piece to close—when or how the prospect will buy, not *if* he or she will buy. When you close throughout the presentation, the "if he or she will buy" has already been answered.

Close each step of your sales process just as you would the order at the end of the presentation. Close the customer on being the decision maker. Ask the prospect directly about the authority to make the decision and where it resides. This is an easy question. If the prospect wants literature, ask about the information desired, and what needs to transpire for him or her to take the next step. Close the customer on the next step in the process, whatever it may be. Ask the prospect what decision will be made, and how and when it will be made. This approach will secure your future and control the sale in a way that allows you to easily close the final order when the time comes.

Close on What Is Important to the Customer

Closing is ineffective when we don't recognize the prospect's needs. No matter how much importance you put on your product or services, the prospect is going to part with cash only if he or she sees a benefit. Selling benefits is valuable only if the customer thinks the features you emphasize are in fact benefits. Take the example of someone coming to buy a car. If as a salesperson you harp on your ability to give the customer a good price when she is looking for just the right car, you may miss the opportunity to make a sale because you never find out what the customer is really trying to buy.

Besides closing regularly and throughout the entire presentation, you must remember to find out what the prospect wants to buy so that you can close on that. This requires that you do your homework during the presentation, asking key questions to determine the most important benefits you can offer to the customer.

Our objective in asking a closing question is to get a positive response. By making sure we ask the prospect to buy what he or she desires, we increase our chances of making the sale. Your product, like others, may not be a perfect fit. The prospect will probably have to give up things he or she likes whatever solution he or she chooses. One product may have better features, another might be more economical—there is always a trade-off. The key in asking your questions is to discover what pieces of the solution you have that the prospect likes, and mention those specifically when you close. This is accomplished by questioning the prospect on the value of the solution. For example:

> **Salesperson:** *Ms. Prospect, you said that you wanted an investment program that had aggressive growth potential. As I have shown you through this prospectus, this fund invests in many start-up companies, which, as you know, provide the largest opportunities for growth of any stocks, wouldn't you agree?*
>
> **Prospect:** *This is perfect; it gives me a chance to increase my assets significantly in the short term, and it will be fun to watch the more volatile movements as it grows.*

This first statement to the prospect verifies her specific interest. Now we ask the question about the value of this benefit.

> **Salesperson:** *Ms. Prospect, tell me again specifically why you want this high growth in your program. And how do you feel about the extra risk necessary to obtain it?*

With these questions, we understand what is important to the prospect and why. Her answer provides the basis for your closing statement.

> **Prospect:** *I have plenty of money in solid, low-risk investments. I need to increase my chances of having extra money at retirement. The last thing I need is another CD.*

With this answer you have the prospect's reason for buying, "she needs/wants something aggressive." When you close, you can now tell her that she should buy because your proposal gives her the aggressive investments she has stated she was looking for.

AVOID GIVING LISTS WHEN CLOSING—THEY'RE SIMPLY BORING!

Lists are simply boring. When closing, it is especially important that you avoid presenting your product and its features as a list. Lists typically focus on features and not benefits. Because their focus is not typically benefits, if you have ever been the recipient of such a list, you know that they are terribly boring, and you can be sure your prospect feels the same way.

Rather than listing your product's features, find out where the prospect's interests lie, then talk about those specific features. Even better, ask the prospect to tell you about how a particular item would be helpful. For example, let's say you're selling cars. As you know from buying a car, there are many different aspects of a car that can be discussed: accessories, handling, power, mileage, style, comfort, and on and on. There are hundreds, if not thousands, of features you could list for the customer. But which ones do you list? Which ones does your customer want to hear about? Unless you ask, you won't have a clue where to begin. Unless you know what the prospect is looking for in a car, you can't even begin. If you ask the question *Ms. Prospect, just what is important to you about your next car?* you can begin with the prospect's interests. If you were to list a number of features for the prospect, you might or might not list features that she was interested in. Thus, by listing features, you have an excellent chance of boring the prospect, something I think we can agree you don't want to do, especially on the telephone.

The best technique for closing is to restate to the customer those specific things that the customer said he or she wanted. The most powerful words the customer will hear are his or her own.

Remember, never assume for the customer what he or she will or won't buy. Many times the things that are important to us in a purchase are of no concern at all to the customer. If you are an investment salesperson two or three years from retirement, your investment concerns are quite different from those of a twenty-year-old just starting a portfolio. What to you seems absolutely unbearable risk may be exciting and worthwhile to a young person. Or you could be talking to someone who has plenty of money and for whom risk is not even a consideration. By making the assumption that he or she wouldn't buy because it's too risky, you may lose the sale.

WHEN SHOULD YOU CLOSE?

There are a number of times when you should close. First, you should close on every offer to buy. In other words, when the prospect says, *I want to buy* or *I need to buy,* you should ask for the order. This often occurs very early in the presentation. For example, you may answer the phone and the person on the other end says, *I need to get another computer.* This buying statement should be closed immediately. You might try, *Did you want to pick that computer up at the store, or should we deliver it?* Yes, it is true, you don't know what computer the prospect wants, but that is not important. What you want to know is, is the prospect going to buy. The answer to that question will tell you. If the prospect says, *I will come in and pick it up,* then you know you have a sale. All you need to do is find out what computer the prospect wants. Most of the time the prospect will say, *Oh, I had a couple of questions first,* and then you can find out specifically what he or she wants.

As you go through your presentation, you should listen carefully for buying statements made by the prospect. Take advantage of these statements to ask a closing question. You may not get the sale each time, but you will become aware of what it is in the prospect's mind that is now preventing him or her from making the decision.

ALWAYS CLOSE SOMETHING!

You must close something in every call, and closing doesn't necessarily mean getting an order. The most important reason for closing something in every call is not, as you might think, to get closer to the sale. Although getting closer to the sale is important, it is more critical that you feel good after each call so that you can make another with all the energy and enthusiasm necessary to be successful. When you don't make progress, it's depressing, and that hurts your next effort.

Another important aspect of closing something in every call is knowing that you are not wasting your time with the prospect. If you make five or six calls to a prospect and never make any headway, that may be a sign that you need to lower the priority on calling that person and instead call someone new who might be more interested. Selling is a series of tasks that make a complete sale—make sure you complete at least one new task in your call.

Remember, if you didn't get closer to the sale, you probably got farther away! When you finish each call, you should notice your progress. If you are keeping records of your actions, it will be obvious if you have made any gains, because you will be entering them into the customer's information. If you have not, you should consider why you are calling and if the time might be better spent with another prospect.

WHEN NOTHING IS HAPPENING

We often get into an account and find that we just can't get the prospect to move forward. Other times we are working with an account who just seems to be putting us off over and over again. Before you give up on such accounts, you might try asking the prospect specifically what you need to do to get the business. For example, *Ms. Dudley, we have been chatting now for the past couple of weeks and you have always given me encouragement that you might be able to use my services. What can I do at this point to make something happen?*

ALWAYS CLOSE WITH BENEFITS

My experience in sales has told me that a lot of people don't really know what a benefit is. In fact, most salespeople rarely use benefits; they use advantages and call them benefits. You hear salespeople all the time saying, *The benefit of our product is our lifetime warranty* or *The benefit of our service is that we have the best on-time record.* These may or may not be benefits.

A benefit is a combination of two factors. The first is the prospect's request for a specific feature or advantage. The second is your proper presentation of that advantage to the prospect. Thus, if during your presentation your prospect said, *I really need to have on-time deliveries,* the statement above, *The benefit of our service is that we have the best on-time record,* would be a benefit if it were presented properly.

The correct form for a benefit statement is to say to the prospect, *Mr. Prospect, you said that one of the most important things to you was on-time delivery. The benefit of our service is that we have the best on-time delivery record in the industry.* This statement reflects the prospect's desire for the specific advantage in question, and thus it becomes a most powerful statement.

The key to closing sales is selling the customer exactly what he or she wants, at least to the best of our ability. When you use benefits to close the sale, you are selling the customer exactly what he or she has requested. Obviously, this increases your chances of making the sale.

ALWAYS CLOSE FOR MORE THAN YOU THINK YOU WILL GET

When you were a kid, if you asked your dad for a dollar, you might get the dollar, but you were not likely to get more. This is also true of your prospects and customers. When you ask for an order, if you don't ask for the maximum the customer will buy, you very well may leave money on the table. Like your dad, prospects probably will not make the extra effort to offer more than you have asked for; if they do, you know you have made a serious error in your determination of their needs.

Preparation, again, is the key to making a good offer. As you work with the prospect, you must carefully determine what her or his real needs are. When the offer is correct for the customer, you have the best chance of making the sale. When you don't offer enough, or offer too much, the opportunity for the offers of competitors to look better than yours is great. Let me give you a real-life example from my own experience. When I joined Logitech, the sales team was selling new resellers on the idea of buy one and get one free—one to show and one to go, as we called it. I was quite aware that dealers would accept this offer all day long. Although it was not supposed to be offered to the same dealer more than once, you can bet that was happening. If I was going to increase sales, I had to ditch this offer, and quick. My solution was based on the fact that I knew the dealers were selling computers and that most of the computers they sold had to have a mouse. Additionally, other people who had computers were going to be buying mice for their older computers (this was still the beginning of the mouse industry), and the dealers would be selling additional mice there as well. My plan was to trick the salespeople into asking for more, as it was logical that the dealers needed more, and given the option would buy more. I implemented the following rule: *You can give the dealer a free mouse and any software that goes with the purchased mice as long as the dealer buys as least five mice. For orders of less than five, you will need my signature to send a free one.* This strategy worked quite well. Although the salespeople grumbled at first, they soon found, as I already knew they would, that in most cases, the dealers didn't have any problem purchasing five mice. The reason for this was obvious: In most cases they were selling more than that anyway, and they needed the mice. After the salespeople recovered from the traumatic experience of having to ask for such a large order, I suggested to them that if they would simply find out how many mice the reseller sells in a month and offer 75 percent of that quantity, they would probably get even larger orders. With a bit of hesitation, they tried, and the rest is history. Our sales skyrocketed.

I repeated this same success just last year with a software company that asked for my assistance. Asking for the right size order is key. If you ask for too little, you risk not filling the customer's needs, and if you ask for too much, you may chase the customer away. By asking for what the customer really needs and wants, you look more professional and make it easier for the customer to accept.

Find out what the customer really needs and then, in your

closing statement, make two offers. The first offer should be what you think is right for the customer, and the second just a bit more. In the mouse story, we accomplished this by asking the customer how many mice were sold per month. If the customer said five, we then made the following offer:

> **Salesperson:** *Mr. Reseller, based on the fact that you sell five mice per month, we would normally ask you to get about eight units, which is enough for you to get through the next thirty days without a problem, even if there are a couple of extra sales. However, if you don't feel you could sell those in a reasonable time, you could just get five to start. Which would be better for you, to start with eight or five?*

The response was surprising: Often the resellers would ask for even more than we offered. They knew by the way we presented the sale that we were trying to make things more convenient for them and also make them successful. With the other benefits we offered, they would sometimes decide to order even more than we thought they could sell. I suspect that they often lied about their needs in the early dealings, but when they became more comfortable with the company, they would step up to the plate and work with us.

This offer method works extremely well because it is based on the customer's needs and desires. It strengthens the closing statement because it offers the customer two reasonable options. The customer is now thinking which way to buy instead of whether to buy.

An Interesting Set of Sales Calls

I would like to conclude this chapter with a pair of calls that are tied together and illustrate the power of a great presentation voice (which you unfortunately won't get to hear) and a go-for-the-throat attitude closing.

Let me first say that these calls, especially the first, possess a delivery by the salesperson that is full of energy and positive tone. As you will see in the call, the salesperson is able to avoid a number of gigantic land mines with pure energy. By all rights, these calls could have been a complete disaster. Let's take a look.

1.	*Seller:*	Hello. This is Betty Salesperson with ABC Technologies in Jacksonville, Florida.
2.	*Prospect:*	Hi Betty, this is Abe Customer, how are you?
3.	*Seller:*	Great, Abe. How are you doing?
4.	*Prospect:*	Very good, thanks, and you?
5.	*Seller:*	Good, happy Monday to you!
6.	*Prospect:*	Thanks!

Even without hearing the voices, you can tell the salesperson is energized, and the prospect is responding. Keep in mind as you listen to this presentation that the seller is delivering a very positive, upbeat presentation.

7.	*Seller:*	Um . . . you were surfing our Web page here a week or two ago. You downloaded a copy of our MFG manufacturing software.
8.	*Prospect:*	Yeah, I actually did it three times.
9.	*Seller:*	I didn't know it was that much fun to download software. [Laughs]
10.	*Prospect:*	Yeah, really. I had tried to unzip the files, and it might have been an older version of Superzip, but it didn't work.
11.	*Seller:*	Uh huh.
12.	*Prospect:*	Then I downloaded a new version of Quickzip and that, but I still had problems. Are you in tech support or sales?
13.	*Seller:*	Sales.
14.	*Prospect:*	OK.

Note that even though the conversation is negative, the salesperson is having a good time. The buyer has just had major problems downloading the software, yet the seller stays positive.

15. *Seller:*	But I'm intelligent, so keep going.	
16. *Prospect:*	Well, I had a problem. I was on the phone with tech support 'cause I couldn't get it to work at one of my accounts.	
17. *Seller:*	Oh, you've already been with our tech support.	
18. *Prospect:*	In fact, tech support is supposed to call me back, but they haven't.	
19. *Seller:*	What you downloaded you took to the customer?	
20. *Prospect:*	Yeah.	
21. *Seller:*	OK, what's the nature of the symptom?	
22. *Prospect:*	Well, um, when I, the software loads, but I can't, I can't run the link to it.	
23. *Seller:*	Uh huh . . .	
24. *Prospect:*	'Cause it locks up software, and I get a database error . . .	
25. *Seller:*	Uh huh.	
26. *Prospect:*	Trying to attach to the MFG database . . .	
27. *Seller:*	OK.	
28. *Prospect:*	So, he's supposed to call me back 'cause the customer's upset, 'cause you know . . .	
29. *Seller:*	Of course . . .	

Again, the prospect is having a bad time with the seller's products, but the salesperson stays positive and agrees with the problems.

30. *Prospect:*	They're not a . . .	
31. *Seller:*	Let me ask you a question. Does the customer already have the demo MFG software out there?	
32. *Prospect:*	Yeah.	
33. *Seller:*	OK, um, and this is like an imminent purchase. This is very serious customer, this is not just a . . .	

This is key to any close: You must qualify the customer. Here, the seller confirms that the sale is possible.

34. *Prospect:* Well. It's a trail. If they like it, they're going to buy it.
35. *Seller:* Well, of course, of course. Ah, OK, good.
36. *Prospect:* So . . .
37. *Seller:* And in the short term?
38. *Prospect:* What?
39. *Seller:* Like, we get it up and running, they take a look at it . . .

Further qualification, and now she closes.

40. *Prospect:* Yeah.
41. *Seller:* Then in a couple of weeks, they're going to buy it? OK, I was saying we can help you sell the program to your customer. Unfortunately, you downloaded an older version, so when tech support gets back with you, they might say you need the current version. I have a suggestion to make your life easier.
42. *Prospect:* Uh huh.

The positive mood of the call has drawn the prospect in.

43. *Seller:* If you would be willing to put a copy of MFG software on your credit card, I'll send you a copy of the product, and if for some reason the customer doesn't like it, I guarantee we'll be happy to take it back. On the other hand, if you want to keep it on your shelf for your next deal or want to convert it to a store demo copy, that would be fine, too. Why don't you slap it on a card, so we can send you a new copy you can take out to your customer—the latest version, manuals, support disks—load it up, if you have any trouble.

Because of the positive nature of the presentation, the salesperson is able to ask a buyer, who has yet to say a positive thing about the product, for an order! Amazing. Even more incredible, you will see that the prospect's answer is positive.

44. **Prospect:** How much is it, anyway?
45. **Seller:** Which product is it for?
46. **Prospect:** MFG Extended.
47. **Seller:** OK. Extended. How many users?
48. **Prospect:** Oh, twenty.
49. **Seller:** OK. Twenty users. That's $1,450 retail. Your price is 40 percent off that, which is $870 plus $15 shipping and handling.
50. **Prospect:** I can't authorize the purchase. I'll need to get the sales manager to do that.

We see here two more surprises and potential disasters. The seller failed to qualify the prospect early in the call and is now finding out that he is not the decision maker.

51. **Seller:** OK. Have you installed one of these before or is this your first time?
52. **Prospect:** Well, I'll be honest with you, a couple of years ago we tried MFG Runner.
53. **Seller:** Uh huh . . .
54. **Prospect:** And I installed that at a couple of sites. Then we found a couple of customers were having problems. It was very problematic.
55. **Seller:** Uh huh.
56. **Prospect:** We had a lot of problems with the database portion of the program, and I lost two accounts because of it.
57. **Seller:** I hope you will let me make it up to you. That first version of the product did have some problems.
58. **Prospect:** Because; let me finish . . .
59. **Seller:** OK, sorry . . .
60. **Prospect:** Because of all these problems with the database freezing, the customer had a big investment in software and hardware, and with all the problems he was having . . .

61. *Seller:*	Right.
62. *Prospect:*	We couldn't resolve the problem.
63. *Seller:*	Uh huh.
64. *Prospect:*	It was problematical, and it locked up the database. They couldn't run the system efficiently, so we stopped selling the product.
65. *Seller:*	I see.
66. *Prospect:*	You know how it is, as consultants and re-sellers, we can't have those kinds of major issues.
67. *Seller:*	Absolutely, I totally agree.
68. *Prospect:*	So, I figured three years later, you would have new products.
69. *Seller:*	Right, and we do.
70. *Prospect:*	So here I am, back again. But I'm a bit discouraged. It looks like the same problems.

The last ten or so lines of the conversation reveal the second problem: The prospect has actually done business before with complete dissatisfaction. Again, the seller all throughout has stayed very positive and seems to be carrying the prospect along.

71. *Seller:*	I don't think so. It's probably your old version or a setup problem. The new version is almost, except for the interface and function, completely rewritten.
72. *Prospect:*	Uh huh.
73. *Seller:*	Could you authorize a $650 store copy?

Another close! Incredible! This is what I mean: You must continue to close all the way through the conversation. The seller is closing a prospect who has said that the product didn't work in the past, that it lost him business, and that it looks like it doesn't work now. But if you could hear the voices, you would discover that even though the prospect is complaining, the seller and the prospect are in very good moods, a tone set and maintained by the salesperson early on in the call. He has even closed again when the prospect just said he can't authorize the order.

74. **Prospect:** I could have Wes authorize it.
75. **Seller:** Do you want me to give Wes a call? Oh, you're in the office. Is he available?
76. **Prospect:** So you think I should load the store copy on their machines?
77. **Seller:** Sure, take the store copy, which is the latest version, and load it up for them.
78. **Prospect:** Yeah.
79. **Seller:** You'll need to make sure that you remove any existing copies from the machine first, you know, de-install anything of our stuff that might already be on there.

Now that the prospect is following, the salesperson stops asking for the order and starts discussing what should be done (assumptive closing).

80. **Prospect:** I've already deleted the whole directory and . . .
81. **Seller:** Good. You're going to be receiving a real production copy with serial numbers and everything, and then if you have a problem . . .
82. **Prospect:** Uh huh . . .
83. **Seller:** Call me from the customer's site, and I will walk to tech support if I can't help you get it running properly.

Closing again. The seller is simply assuming the buyer will follow the directions. The buyer now responds by looking for the decision maker without even being asked.

84. **Prospect:** Uh . . . hold on a sec. Let me see if I can get Wes.
85. **Seller:** All right.
86. **Prospect:** Great, thanks.
87. **Seller:** OK.
88. **Prospect:** Wes is in a meeting now, but I can take the information down.

89. *Seller:*	OK.
90. *Prospect:*	I'll have him get in touch with you.
91. *Seller:*	That's great! I can call back and ask for Wes in a bit. I just need a credit card, you know, so I can ship you the store copy.

Once again the salesperson closes the deal.

92. *Prospect:*	OK.
93. *Seller:*	And what I'm going to ship you is a twenty-user MFG Extended.
94. *Prospect:*	OK.
95. *Seller:*	Don't even worry about messing with the stuff you downloaded.
96. *Prospect:*	Um . . .
97. *Seller:*	You can use the box we're going to send you for all your future presentations of the product.
98. *Prospect:*	Super . . . and I'll let Wes know what's going on.

The seller spent the last couple of lines telling the prospect again that he is going to order and receive this product. The prospect, in his last statement, now indicates he will close the decision maker.

99. *Seller:*	I'll give him an hour, and maybe catch him before he leaves today?
100. *Prospect:*	Yeah, that's good.
101. *Seller:*	Great, thanks, Abe.
102. *Prospect:*	OK.
103. *Seller:*	Don't worry, we'll take good care of your customer. And one more thing about your old customers . . .
104. *Prospect:*	Yeah?
105. *Seller:*	I'm going to get back to you and see if I can help out with some of those old customers once this situation is resolved. Maybe I'll

		be able to bring you some new ones to make up for the past.
106.	*Prospect:*	OK.
107.	*Seller:*	OK. Thanks, Abe.
108.	*Prospect:*	All right.
109.	*Seller:*	Bye-bye.
110.	*Prospect:*	Thank you.

With a couple of pats on the back, the seller leaves the phone. This call is an excellent example of concept *"you must always be closing"* if you wish to succeed. The call is full of errors by the salesperson, but the combination of a very positive attitude and relentless closing appears to have worked.
* * End of call * *

This is really a very unusual call. I have been working with salespeople for years and have run into few calls where the salesperson is so relentless in making something happen. Even more exciting is the follow-up call with Wes. Let's take a look.

1.	*Secretary:*	Resellers Are Us. Good afternoon.
2.	*Seller:*	Good afternoon. Wes, please.
3.	*Secretary:*	May I ask who's calling?
4.	*Seller:*	Betty Salesperson with ABC Technologies.
5.	*Secretary:*	One moment, Betty, thank you.
6.	*Prospect:*	Hello?
7.	*Seller:*	Hi, Wes. This is Betty Salesperson with ABC Technologies in Jacksonville, Florida.
8.	*Prospect:*	Yes, Betty. I was expecting your call.
9.	*Seller:*	Oh, great. I'm not interrupting you, am I?
10.	*Prospect:*	No.
11.	*Seller:*	Good. Did Abe call you?
12.	*Prospect:*	Yes. He said that we're getting a store copy of MFG Extended.

Look at that: Wes has already been closed by our buddy Abe.

13.	**Seller:**	Yes, that's right, and this is for the customer he is already working with, who has been

		having a problem. But afterwards, you'll be able to use this copy with other customers.
14.	*Prospect:*	OK. And what is the name of your company, Betty?
15.	*Seller:*	ABC Technologies.
16.	*Prospect:*	OK.
17.	*Seller:*	Are you familiar with us?
18.	*Prospect:*	Yes.
19.	*Seller:*	Great.
20.	*Prospect:*	OK. Let me make sure you're in the company's database here.
21.	*Seller:*	Great. Wes, I didn't get it from Abe. What's your position there?
22.	*Prospect:*	Manager of sales and customer service.
23.	*Seller:*	Excellent! What's left? [laughs]
24.	*Prospect:*	Oh, a bunch of stuff. [laughs]
25.	*Seller:*	And I'm your rep. So if you would just put my name in the database for future reference. . . .

After checking the address information, the buyer quickly gave the seller the order she was after. It is obvious that the positive attitude of the salesperson on Abe influenced him to commit Wes to the deal. All in all, a great example of closing.

Unfortunately, as we said before, you could not hear the wonderful positive attitude of the salesperson and how it takes over the call. But even without hearing this for yourself, you can see it in the multiple closing questions asked even under the most inauspicious circumstances. The only way you can close in a situation like that is to carry the customer through the negatives, and this is exactly what Betty did in this call.

What Have We Learned?

- Closing is not just asking for the order.
- Preparation is the key to effective closing.
- Close each issue, transaction, and task of your presentation as you go.
- Close only on the customer's wants.

- Avoid using lists in closing, as they usually focus on features rather than benefits.
- Always close using benefit statements giving the prospect two or more options to buy.
- Close on more rather than less.

Practice

1. Just for fun, take a look at the sales calls we have analyzed in this book. Most of them are actual calls with the names changed. You will notice the lack of closing questions throughout. Make tapes of some of your own calls and look for the closing opportunities you have in the calls. Try to develop some closing scenarios that you can use in your calls.
2. What is the most important thing to remember about closing?
3. What is a trial close?
4. When should you close?
5. Construct a benefit closing statement.

[*Sample answers to these exercises appear in the Appendix.*]

Hints for Improving

1. Practice trial closing.
2. Think about your calls before you dial. Look at what you know about the customer and what you believe you can close.
3. Practice listening for those innocent buying statements made by customers.
4. Learn to ask quality closing questions and wait for the answers.

TEN

BRINGING IT TOGETHER; CONTROLLING THE CALL

What Is the Goal?

The goal of your effort is to control the sales call and the prospect. You want to guide the prospect down the road that leads to an intelligent decision to buy your product or service. To attain this goal, you must accomplish a number of things:

1. Develop a relationship with the prospect.
2. Gain the prospect's trust and confidence.
3. Discover the prospect's true needs.
4. Educate the prospect on the (your) solution.
5. Get the prospect to make a buying decision.

As we have seen, accomplishing these tasks on the telephone is more difficult than it might be in person, because we lack so many tools of presentation and communication on the telephone. We have learned that the telephone is a completely different selling environment from face-to-face and that it requires some special attention if we are to be successful.

This book has tried to point out those things you must do in every telephone call if you wish to be successful. Each will help you to make a better-quality call and give you more success. Let's take a minute to review.

In Chapter 2 we discuss the telephone selling environment. If you are going to be successful on the telephone, you must understand its limitations and restrictions. Understanding that a telephone presentation is a commercial and just what that means for how you should proceed is a critical part of making a good presentation. Learning what the lack of vision means in terms of seeing your prospect's environment or reactions to you allows you to compensate for these weaknesses. Understanding the difficulties present in telephone communication will allow you to make your presentation more effective.

In Chapter 3 we discuss how your energy must be transmitted in a positive way and the effects that has on each call. Your voice is the sizzle of your sale, and constantly maintaining an excited, passionate, and colorful presentation must become second nature to you. You must always remember that whatever your emotional state during the sales call, it will be transmitted

132

across the telephone. If you want your prospect to get excited about you, your company, and its products, you must show that excitement yourself. Your mood and attitude are contagious. Your casual voice is completely ineffective in making such a presentation.

In Chapter 4 we discuss specifically the fact that your voice is your primary presentation tool and how you can use it to be more effective. Understanding the telephone selling environment is the first critical part of a successful telephone presentation. Your presentation of the information makes a difference in how that information is perceived. This ingredient of the sales call is all-encompassing in its effect. Whether you are investigating the prospect's business or answering an objection, your presentation of the material, your attitude, your mood, your passion is being transmitted to the prospect and affecting how he or she responds. All of this is coming directly from how you use your voice.

These three chapters of the book really make up the presentation aspect of your sales effort. In combination, they give you the sharp and colorful presentation you need to move the prospect to a positive environment in which you can have a solid relationship.

In Chapter 5 we cover the first aspect of selling, both on and off the telephone: finding the decision maker. We discuss the dangers of not talking to the decision maker and how important it is to understand just what decision-making authority this decision maker has. We explain the value and dangers of talking to NERDs and how important it is that we not upset or anger anyone we talk to in an organization. Remember, no matter how good your presentation or products are, if you don't convince the decision maker, you're not going to make the sale. As we have seen, it is hard for a NERD to handle this task for you; you must find the decision maker.

Adding this key ingredient to your presentation, you will now find yourself making passionate presentations to the person who counts. If we accomplish nothing else in this book, this will increase your sales results. By adding the right attitude and always finding the decision maker, you give yourself the opportunity to make a presentation of your product or service. This is absolutely necessary if you are going to make a sale.

In Chapter 6 we discuss the techniques of qualifying. Qualifying is not just asking if a company buys the products or services you sell and if the person you are talking to is the decision maker. Qualifying is the process of closing each step of the presentation, so that you can successfully move to the next step. Qualifying is the key to setting the next step in the call, and it is important to have a next step in every call if you want to be efficient and successful in your effort.

With the decision maker in front of you and your massive positive energy, you now add the qualification. Qualification allows you to make progress, to understand what the decision maker needs and wants. It allows you to know when the decision maker is ready to move on to the next aspect of the presentation and whether you have successfully answered the last objection. Handled properly, the stated ingredients let you make the passionate presentation you need to be successful, let you make it to the right person, and let you make closure of each step of your effort.

In Chapter 7 we cover the structure of a presentation. Every sale has certain requirements that must be fulfilled if the sale is to be successful. These tasks must be made part of your presentation and should be broken down into smaller tasks that you can use as a guide to your presentation of the material to the decision maker. From this chapter you now have a method by which you can develop a highly effective presentation to guide you in your selling efforts.

In Chapter 8 we talk about the nature of curiosity and its importance in maximizing opportunities in the sales effort. We talk about the clues and open doors that prospects so often present, and how you must relentlessly pursue them if you are to be successful. It is important to listen to what the prospect doesn't say as much as to what he or she does say to find opportunities in the sale.

Finally, in Chapter 9, we talk about closing and how important it is to close and close effectively. We learn again about the importance of closing not just the final order but each step and task of our presentation. We learn about the usefulness of trial closes and how they bring us closer to the prospect's real needs. Closing is not something you can leave to the end of your presentation. To be effective, you must close throughout the presentation.

These are the key ingredients to making a sale on the telephone. As you learn to put them together, you will find your success increasing. You will find the telephone more fun and easier to use effectively. It won't be because you know your product better, but because you're using your current knowledge more effectively.

THE CONTROL OF THE CALL

As we stated at the beginning of this chapter, your goal is to control the prospect and the sales call. A quick look at the ingredients we have suggested will show how you now better control the whole process of your telephone sales situation.

We start with your attitude and presentation. By adding energy to your presentation, you start controlling the prospect from your first words. You have an impact on the tone of the call—hopefully a very positive one. Whether you get a prospect who is already excited or one who is defensive, your positive emotional package will be delivered in your first efforts to gain the prospect's friendship and trust. The maintenance of your positive attitude will continue to pressure the prospect toward a positive response. This is the beginning of your control over the prospect during the call.

Finding the decision maker is the key to controlling the sales process. Unless you completely understand the decision-making process and know the authority of your decision maker, you cannot control the sale. Talking to the decision maker enables you to control the sale as it progresses while understanding the real needs as only the decision maker can reveal them.

Qualifying now brings you the ability to master and complete each task of the sales process. By qualifying each task in your sales effort, you can safely move through the successive steps of your sales presentation.

The setting of call objectives allows you to carefully plan

out your presentation. Additionally, your sales task list lets you know exactly what needs to be accomplished to make the sale, and provides the order in which these things must be accomplished.

Your curiosity and investigation assists you in developing the maximum number of opportunities within the call. Your investigation of open doors and other opportunities implied by the prospect helps you to expand your knowledge of the situation and avoid potential land mines not immediately visible to you.

Closing is the key to selling. If you don't close, you won't sell. Closing relentlessly throughout your presentation allows you to know exactly where in the sales process you are, which tasks are complete, and which still need to be completed. By closing as you proceed through the tasks, you assure yourself the opportunity to close the sale at the end of the call without a significant number of objections or problems.

Together, all of these factors give you a presentation that is dependent only on your ability to solve the prospect's problems effectively with your products or services. By controlling the prospect's mood, you gain the relationship you need to be successful. Add to the positive mood the ability to control the sales process and you have the best chance of making the sale. You only need to make sure you qualify and close at every opportunity as you complete each of your sales tasks and the sale will be yours.

TAPE TRAINING: A METHOD FOR IMPROVING YOUR SKILLS

Tape training, although a little bit uncomfortable at first, will be one of your best friends in your attempt to improve your skills. I personally credit my work with tapes in the magazine business for my high level of skill today, both as a salesperson and as a sales trainer. Tape training taught me how to understand the sales call and how to listen to the prospect, and, most important, it gave me a way to discover my own weaknesses and strengths. If you do nothing else after reading this book, simply listen to some of your own sales calls on a regular basis. The rewards from this activity will be enormous.

You will need a couple of items in order to make tape training work. First, you will need a cassette recorder that has a mike jack, a counter, and a pause control, and voice activation is also nice to have. Next, you will need some cassette tapes; I prefer the sixty-minute tapes. These tapes do not have to be of high quality, as you will be recording only voice on them. Finally, you will need a recording jack that allows you to record both sides of your sales calls. There are a variety of jacks available, but I have found the best to be those that hook between the handset or headset and the telephone; there seem to be fewer compatibility problems, and they make excellent recordings. When using the tape with your own sales calls and for your own learning, you should not run into problems, but it is recommended that you find out the regulations for hooking the device to your telephone just in case.

Before you start your program, you should make a couple of calls to friends and test your equipment. You want to make sure before you start taping your sales calls that the equipment makes a recording that you can hear and that you don't have to fuss with the equipment during the call because you aren't sure of its operation. The fewer distractions, the better.

Taping Your Calls

Once you're up to speed with your equipment and everything is in working order, you are ready to start taping your calls. I suggest that you start by taping your prospecting calls, as those typically have the most potential for education. I have found that when taping, especially when you're just starting out, it is best to just turn the recorder on and let it run—don't try to stop it between calls or monitor its working in any way. You may also want to put the recorder out of your direct line of sight at first so that it doesn't interfere with your confidence during the calls. You will find that if you just let it run, you will forget about it until the tape ends and the machine make a noise. With this idea in mind, you should have a list of calls that need to be made. Typically, I would suggest you have somewhere between thirty and fifty calls to make. The reason for this high number is that you will not contact everyone you call and it may take a number of calls to actually get a call on tape. In addition, you will find it useful to set aside a two-hour time period for your calls. You may even have to turn the tape over during your session.

Your goal should be to get three to five presentations on tape. I would mark in your customer file or sales database that you taped the call, as this reference may be valuable later and for future taping.

Analyzing Your Calls

As we stated earlier, you don't really need an instructor to help you, although if you know someone who has a higher level of skill than yourself, you can certainly invite that person to critique your calls.

Call analysis is really quite simple. As you listen to your calls on the tape, you may find it useful to use the counter on your recorder to mark the beginning of each call. This way, if you decide later that you need to replay a particular call, you can easily find it on the tape. As you listen to your call, listen for anything you can hear that is good or bad about your call and write it down. When making your notes, leave about five or six blank lines between entries so that you have room to make additional comments later. As you go back through this book, you will see a number of topics that you can then compare to your call. Be as critical as you can. Look for as many opportunities as you can to improve your call, whether in the realm of your presentation, your product knowledge, or the way you handled specific situations during the call. Make sure you keep a detailed list of what you find because you will use that list in the next step.

Improving From What You Hear

Now that you have made and analyzed your tapes, you can take advantage of them to train yourself. This is done quite simply by taking each of the errors you made and comparing it to what you believe is correct or what you can find in this book or in others on how to sell successfully.

Now take your list and write down under each opportunity what you might have done instead. If you see a problem and you know what would be better, write that down under your entry. If you are not sure what you should do, you can either seek advice in books on sales or ask someone you know with more experience what he or she would do. Be picky; if you hear a phrase that doesn't sound very good, take the time to rewrite it so that it's better. Then take the time to learn the phrase so that the next time you have the opportunity, you will know exactly what to say.

It is my hope that you have found this book as enjoyable to read as it was fun to write. Just remember: it's not easy to change habits or to implement new techniques. Take your time, and be patient. Trying different techniques as you get the chance, and you will be successful.

APPENDIX

This appendix contains answers and explanations for the exercises at the end of each chapter. We have tried to give you a way to check your attempts to answer the questions.

Before reading the answers, you should make an attempt to understand the question using the material in the chapter, then look at our analysis or answer.

We hope you will find this helpful in implementing the methods and techniques we have suggested in this book.

CHAPTER TWO: THE TELEPHONE AS A SALES TOOL

Challenge

Your challenge was to list some ideas as to the meaning of these statements and the implications they might have for your call.

Don't worry about having the same answers as the book; the idea was for you to think about these things and understand how you might make them happen in your calls. Compare my answers and take note of how you can use the information to improve your own presentation.

These are some of the things you might have listed.

1. *Where does your customer get his or her picture of you?*

- You must remember to tell the prospect about yourself and how you will serve him or her. You should always sell yourself, something that many salespeople forget to do.
- The picture is drawn by how you sound—kids sound different from adults, educated people different from the not educated, and professional people different from nonprofessionals.
- How you sound is a function of your speech, both words and tone.
- How you sound is also a function of your attitude and feelings. If you're positive, you will sound positive; if you're upset, you will most likely sound upset.
- Your overall sound is created by how you approach the call. You make yourself sound good the same way an actor

does: by acting the way you want the prospect to see you. This is the same way you treat a child. To play, you act like a child; to discipline, you act stern—you create the right picture for the child depending on what is to be accomplished.

- In a sales call, you want to sound professional, enthusiastic, and sincere. You want to gain the prospect's respect and confidence. Accomplishing this requires you to act accordingly so that the prospect sees the right picture.

2. *Where does your customer get his or her picture of your product?*

- Once again, your voice is the transmitter of the picture. If your product is to look good, it looks good through your voice. If you're not careful, you can tarnish your product's appearance and appeal.
- What you say about your product is also very important. If you can tell the prospect about those parts of your product he or she is most interested in, it will help to increase the value or quality of the picture he or she receives.

3. *Where does your customer get his or her picture of your company?*

- Just as you must sell yourself, you must sell your company. Too many salespeople never tell the prospect about the company and why he or she has chosen the right place to buy.
- The quality of your presentation comes from how believable and sincere that presentation sounds to the prospect. It is also derived from your own enthusiasm, which is transmitted to the prospect.

4. *Where does your customer get his or her excitement for your product?*

- Unless you have reached a prospect who is just plain excited about buying what you sell, most of the enthusiasm and excitement for your product will have to come from you. It will be your energy that catches the prospect's attention and gets her or him excited about your offer.

- As discussed earlier, excitement is transmitted to the prospect from you. If you aren't excited about the product, it is far more difficult for the prospect to become excited.

5. *Where does all the* sizzle *of your presentation come from?*

- You are the *sizzle* or the *fizzle*. Don't depend on the prospect to get excited and buy. You must create the excitement and transmit it to the prospect if you are going to be successful.
- The conduit for the transmission of your story is your voice. Your voice will follow your attitude and feelings, so if you don't feel it, the prospect won't see it.

What Is Your Biggest Advantage Over Media-Type Commercials?

If you said that you are interactive, you are correct. Your ability to accept immediate feedback from the prospect gives you a great advantage over one-way media commercials, especially when combined with the ability to respond. If a media commercial is irritating or offensive, the advertiser is stuck with that problem until the commercial is pulled or modified. Because you have the ability to accept feedback and respond, you can make adjustments for each specific prospect as needed.

Additionally, the lack of direct communication in media commercials prevents asking for the order on the spot and responding to hesitation or objections by the prospect.

CHAPTER THREE: ENERGY, ENTHUSIASM, AND PASSION

Challenge

For this chapter, you will need to investigate your own business, looking for reasons for being excited or passionate about what you sell. You are not trying to pick out every good thing about your company, just those things that you can feel good about and for which you can begin to develop some enthusiasm.

Practice Exercise 1

For this exercise, you should have made a tape of your sales presentations and/or practice at delivering your message in a positive and enthusiastic way. Let a friend or someone else listen to your tape and see if he or she thinks you sound excited about what you are saying. If not, go back and practice. You are looking for a voice that contains energy and has a smile—a voice that will be fun for prospects and customers to listen to.

Practice Exercise 2

Using a fictitious company, here is an example of what you might have on your list. These represent the best things the company does.

- Best delivery in the industry.
- Excellent service.

Practice Exercise 3

Here are examples:

- Very good quality for the price.
- Largest feature set of all competitive products.

Practice Exercise 4

Our company has very good products for the price. Additionally, we have fast delivery and excellent service. This I can get excited about!

CHAPTER FOUR: VOICE: YOUR PRIMARY WEAPON

Ideas for Your Practice

Since I cannot answer the practice exercises for this chapter, I thought I might point out some of the opportunities and concepts you can work toward.

▪ *Comparing your casual to your presentation voice.* The first thing you should notice is whether your presentation voice is different from your regular or casual voice. Many salespeople are surprised to find that they sound almost exactly the same in their sales and personal calls. This isn't bad if your personal calls are full of energy, enthusiasm, and passion, but this is not the case for most of us.

You might look at your personal calls for key emotions you wish to transmit. For example, in your personal calls you may often have a "smile" in your voice. In a sales presentation, you want an obvious smile; if you can find one in your casual voice, you will have a frame of reference for improving your presentation voice.

Besides listening for the smile and enthusiasm in your presentation voice, listen for the tones that transmit the emotional part of your message. Look to see if you are dropping off when the customer gives you an obstacle. Look for situations where you are sending the wrong message in your tone and even in your words because you are frustrated or upset with the prospect or customer.

Listen to your customers and prospects to see if their tones reflect their moods. See if you can see their reactions to what you say and do in their voices. As you become more proficient, you will be able to use these audio clues to move the prospect or customer to more positive ground.

▪ *Searching for ways to improve your presentation.* Make your search simple; listen to other presenters, find those techniques they use that you like, and try to implement them. Use your recorder to practice. Take techniques from the book that you don't find in your presentation and implement them the same way. Use your friends or coworkers to get feedback on how you have tried to use the different methods and techniques.

▪ *Practicing the tough parts of your sales presentation.* As you practice your techniques, try to find the hardest parts of your presentation to practice on. The tough situations are the ones in which it is most critical that you make a good presentation. Here are a couple of ideas:

1. At the first meeting with the prospect
2. When the prospect says something negative relative to your (sales) relationship
3. In answering an objection
4. In explaining those parts of your offer that are the least positive in nature, or your weaknesses (for example, your price is higher than most)

CHAPTER FIVE: NERDS AND THE DECISION MAKER

Practice Exercise 1

Lay out the typical scenarios for the decision-making process in your business. This would include the titles and relationships of the decision makers you usually talk to. Set a plan for how you will present to the different decision makers.

For an example, I will use the sale of manufacturing robots to industry. In this particular sales process, it is necessary to deal with a number of decision makers at different levels in the decision-making process. I am not an expert in this field, but this will give you an example of how you might lay out your own plan.

The players are:

- **End users.** These are the people who use the robots in the manufacturing process.
- **Line managers.** These managers manage the day-to-day operations and the users of the machines. This responsibility gives them a lot of voice in the selection of equipment.
- **Manufacturing engineers.** These are the designers and maintainers of the manufacturing line in question. They are responsible for the specifications of the manufacturing process and thus would spec the robots into the line.
- **Plant general manager and chief financial officer.** These individuals give the final approval for the systems recommended by the MEs and line managers.

In our sales process, we will talk to all of these people except the plant GM and CFO, as they make the decision based on the proposal of middle management. Our presentation strategy for the different groups would be as follows:

- **End users.** Our presentation to the end users will focus on their hands-on knowledge of what makes things work effectively and safely on the line. This group will be the closest to the problems and challenges of total productivity.
- **Line managers.** This group will be the most knowledgeable about the specific needs of the company based on what the future of manufacturing will be. This group will probably have the most say as to what robots are used. They understand not only the users but the technical requirements of the system.
- **Manufacturing engineers.** These guys are the ones who will test and specify all the equipment. Based on the needs and requirements of the plant, they will be the ones to test the potential robots against the specifications of the factory.

Practice Exercise 2

Develop a series of questions that will qualify the decision maker(s) and the decision-making process for you.

The following are the key questions that I would ask of the different participants:

End Users

1. Are you a user of robots on the manufacturing floor?
2. Which ones do you use?
3. How are you involved in the decision process when new machines are purchased?
4. What are the biggest challenges you see at this point relative to the existing robots?
5. What types of robots would you like to see installed?

Line Managers

1. Do you manage the users of robots on the manufacturing floor?
2. Which robots do you use on your line?
3. How are you involved in the selection of new robots?
4. What will be the critical issues in choosing new robots?
5. How is the recommendation to top management made?
6. What can I do to assist you in discovering the specific needs and opportunities you might have?

Manufacturing Engineers

1. Are you involved in the process of specifying new robots for the line?
2. What kinds of information will you need to choose the right equipment?
3. How do you fit into the overall decision process for the purchase?
4. What are your critical issues concerning the robots and the selection of new equipment?

Practice Exercise 3

Look for questions and statements you can use to avoid making a presentation to a NERD.

You will notice that in each of the examples above, I included a question that will determine how that particular individual fits into the decision process.

CHAPTER SIX: PROPER QUALIFYING

Practice Exercise 1

Here is the phone call you analyzed with annotations as to the qualifying questions that might have been asked.

> **1. Secretary:** ABC Widget Corporation. This is Judy. How can I help you?

   2. *Seller:*   Yes . . . I would like to reach the person in charge of purchasing marketing lists.
   3. *Secretary:* I'll transfer you to the marketing manager.
   4. *Seller:*   Great!

The seller should qualify the transfer and make sure he knows who he should be talking to. Obviously, the marketing manager is a good start, but if you don't know the marketing manager's name, you may talk with someone who is not that person. What if Bob is the marketing manager's administrator—would Rob know? The question that should be asked is, *What is the marketing manager's name?*

   5. *Buyer:* Hello, this is Bob.
   6. *Seller:* Hi, Bob. My name is Rob Goodman with Superlists. How are you doing today?
   7. *Buyer:* Fine. What can I do for you?
   8. *Seller:* Well, as I said, Bob, I'm with Superlists and I just wanted to call and find out whether you folks buy marketing lists for your sales efforts.

The seller was transferred to an unknown person. The secretary said he would be transferred to the marketing manager, but the seller never confirmed it—who is "Bob"? A good question here would be, *Bob, I was transferred by the secretary, who said you are the marketing manager. Is that correct?* Even if Rob had gotten the name, it is still possible that Bob is not the marketing manager—the secretary might have made a mistake.

    Second, Rob is taking a big chance because he doesn't know what Bob knows about his company. Bob may have purchased lists from Superlists before with poor results, which could cause problems later. Rob should qualify his prospect's knowledge of his organization with a question like, *Bob, are you familiar with Superlists?* and on the basis of the response find out what specifically Bob knows about the company.

   9. *Buyer:*   Yes, we sure do.
 10. *Seller:* Just out of curiosity, Bob, what kinds of lists do you buy?

11. *Buyer:*   Well, we typically buy demographic lists of purchasers of gidits and fijits because we find those individuals are likely buyers of our products.

12. *Seller:*   Do you use the telephone or face-to-face selling for your widgets?

The seller didn't qualify the potential of the customer by asking about other lists the company might buy with a question like, *Do you purchase any other types of lists?*

The seller does not know for sure what this person's responsibility in the purchase of these lists is. Somewhere in this early part of the conversation, he needs to ask the question, *Are you responsible for the selection and purchase of these lists?*

13. *Buyer:*   We actually use both. We have an inside sales team that qualifies and sells the lower-end accounts, and we have outside sales reps who follow up on those larger customers that need someone at their site to make the decision.

14. *Seller:*   So you would want lists that had the phone numbers as well as the address information, right?

15. *Buyer:*   Absolutely. Without the phone numbers, it takes too much work and time to find the prospect.

16. *Seller:*   Well, we are one of the best list compilation companies in the business and currently one of the top five companies from which you could buy your lists. We have very extensive lists for both gidit and fijit buyers, including some new international lists.

17. *Buyer:*   That sounds good. Why don't you send me the information on your lists so I can take a look at it?

18. *Seller:*   I'd be happy to; would you give me your address?

The seller needs to find out what the prospect wants to look at. This is a typical mistake in telephone selling. You must find out what the prospect is going to do with the information, what information he or she really wants, and how he or she will make a decision.

> **19.** *Buyer:* Our address is . . .
> **20.** *Seller:* Great. I will send it out and give you a call back.
> **21.** *Buyer:* Thanks. Bye.

The seller didn't qualify the next step: What the next call is about, and when it should take place. When the follow-up call comes, he will have to start over because he doesn't have any commitment from the buyer.

> **22.** *Seller:* Bye.

Practice Exercise 2

When reviewing calls, the first thing to look for is if you missed a qualification the first time. In other words: Did you have to go backwards later in the call because you didn't get the information the first time? A common example of this is the qualification of the decision maker. If you got to the end of your call only to discover you aren't talking to the decision maker, then you missed the qualification. If, when you close, the prospect says: "Oh, I need to check out the competition," then you didn't qualify his or her intent to buy before closing. These are the easiest things to spot.

As you listen to your tape, see if you feel that more information would have benefitted you. If you asked the prospect about his business, did he tell you everything that would be valuable to your sales effort? If not, maybe the opportunity for you to qualify better existed.

You will find that the more you listen and learn, the more you will see opportunities even in your best calls.

CHAPTER SEVEN: CALL OBJECTIVES AND THEIR IMPORTANCE

Practice Exercise 1:

Look at the plan that was developed in the Chapter 5 Appendix section (under Practice Exercise 1) for a manufacturing call, and use that plan to analyze your own call.

Practice Exercise 2:

Take your own sales call and list the objectives you should be pursuing in your calls.

In your objectives you should look for the following:

1. Did you make a complete list of those things that are necessary for the sale to be completed? This might include information about the products the customer will need, budget, delivery, service, volume, and scheduling.
2. Did you look for the relationships among the different needs, which are the most important and in what order must they be accomplished?

Practice Exercise 3:

Give the primary reasons call objectives are important.

- Call objectives are important primarily to maintain control and direction in the call.
- Every call has a time limit, and without adherence to objectives, you may run out of time.
- Call objectives help to guide you through your presentation and keep you from missing important issues before you attempt to close.

Practice Exercise 4:

What is a call objective?

A call objective is simply a group of tasks that need to be

accomplished to make the sale. For example: Qualifying the prospect is a call objective, for which the tasks might be (1) determine the decision maker, (2) determine if he or she and the company can use your product or service, and (3) discover what the decision-making process is.

CHAPTER EIGHT: PERSISTENT CURIOSITY AND INVESTIGATION

Practice

Here is our analysis of the call's investigative opportunities.

1. *Secretary:*	This is AVI. May I help you?
2. *Salesperson:*	Yes, I want to talk to Tod in human resources, but first can I get the spelling of his last name, please?
3. *Secretary:*	Sure. It's Hickman, that's H-I-C-K-M-A-N.
4. *Salesperson:*	Great! Is he in, please?

This would have been a good place to find out the real responsibilities of the individual you are trying to reach. By asking the secretary about his title, you could possibly have confirmed his position.

5. *Secretary:*	I'll ring, thank you.
6. *Salesperson:*	Thank you.
7. *Prospect:*	Tod Hickman.
8. *Salesperson:*	Tod, this is Bob Salesman calling from ABC Staffing. How are you doing?
9. *Tod:*	OK.
10. *Salesperson:*	Good. We're a technical contracting service, and we specialize in MIS placements, and I was just a little curious about what type of contractor usage you have at AVI, and if your . . .
11. *Tod:*	We're trying to phase out all the contractors to the greatest extent possible. We're in a very, very rapid growth mode; I've

		hired eighty-five people in the last ten months and a . . .
12.	*Salesperson:*	My goodness . . .

This statement certainly is in conflict with your goals. There are a number of key questions that should be asked, the first being, *Why are contractors being phased out?* Second, Tod said *phased out,* not *we don't use them anymore,* so it would be appropriate to ask where he sees a continued need at this time. This call was the result of a referral, which also deserves investigation. The person who referred you obviously assumed that the need for temps in the technical support area existed. This needs to be investigated.

Another question that might be useful here is *Who else have you been using?*

13.	*Tod:*	. . . and we need 'em periodically, but for the most part we have probably five in our whole company.

Obviously, here we should ask, *Where are they?*

14.	*Salesperson:*	I see.
15.	*Tod:*	. . . so we're not looking to put on any contractors.
16.	*Salesperson:*	I see. Do you think it would be OK if I sent some information just for backup, in case you run into some problems?
17.	*Tod:*	That's fine.
18.	*Salesperson:*	OK, good. Are you still at 123 Ban Street?
19.	*Tod:*	Right.
20.	*Salesperson:*	OK, good enough. And your exact title is manager of human resources?
21.	*Tod:*	Director of human services.
22.	*Salesperson:*	Director of . . . I'm glad I asked. OK, typically what type of contractors do you use when you need them?

This is a good question, and as you will see, there are some possibilities that would have been missed if Bob hadn't investigated the statement *We are phasing out all contractors.* Also important here is to discover if Tod is the only person in the company who might hire these contractors.

23. *Tod:*		Um, systems administrators, um, could be DBAs but primarily systems administrators.
24. *Salesperson:*		Right, OK, well, that is right along our lines.
25. *Tod:*		Unix background, that kind of stuff.

It might be valuable here to ask again if there are any needs. The prospect's earlier statements reflect a possible attempt to dodge the sales call with a simple objection. This is evident by the change in the prospect's response to the questions of usage of contractors in the last couple of statements.

26. *Salesperson:*		Exactly. Well, that's what we specialize in.
27. *Tod:*		Um.
28. *Salesperson:*		What department is usually the one who uses those?
29. *Tod:*		Um . . . MIS . . . the MIS department.
30. *Salesperson:*		And when you do use contractors, it would be coordinated by you?
31. *Tod:*		Yes.

Although the prospect has stated that he has the responsibility for the hiring of contractors, it might be valuable to investigate the possibility of talking to the manager of MIS to see if there are some upcoming needs. It is possible that the HR person is not aware of the MIS department's plans in this area.

32. *Salesperson:*		OK, good enough. Let me get this information off to you, and then I'll follow up to make sure it got there.
33. *Tod:*		Thank you.
34. *Salesperson:*		Thanks for your time, Tod.

35. *Tod:*   Bye.
36. *Salesperson:*   Bye-bye.

The salesperson in this call missed quite a few opportunities to investigate the situation. Without the answers to these questions, you would expect to be stopped in your effort to make the sale, as happened in this call.

CHAPTER NINE : CLOSING

Practice Exercise 1

Just for fun, take a look at the sales calls we have analyzed in this book. Most of them are actual calls with the names changed. You will notice the lack of closing questions throughout. Make tapes of some of your own calls and look for the closing opportunities you have in the calls. Try to develop some closing scenarios that you can use in your calls.

Some of the things you might look for in your calls and your attempt to build some sales scenarios are as follows:

1. Look for transactions, places where you or the prospect asks the other to complete a task. Did you close that task?
2. Look for the next step in any transaction. Did you close the next step?
3. Did you develop some trial closes based on conversations that are likely to come up in your call?
4. Is your close based on finding out what the prospect needs?
5. Does your close have an offer of two logical solutions?

Practice Exercise 2

What is the most important thing to remember about closing?

The most important thing about closing is that it should be practiced constantly, not just when asking for the order.

Practice Exercise 3

What is a trial close?

> A trial close is a test of the prospect's willingness to buy. It is not necessarily based on his or her readiness or specific needs, but more on the assumption that since he or she is talking to you, the potential is there. Trial closes help the seller find out where the buyer is standing.

Practice Exercise 4

When should you close?

> Obviously, all the time, but specifically, in answer to any question or objection, in response to any buying statement, as a test when presenting a benefit, in response to any transaction, and to set up the next step in any situation.

Practice Exercise 5

Construct a benefit closing statement.

> Ms. Prospect, you said you wanted A and B and that they are both very important to your decision, correct? Great; our solution includes both A and B. Based on your needs, I would say you should get solution one, or would solution two be better for you?

I hope these exercises have helped you to better understand the material in this book. Feel free to use the answers given here as models for your calls and practice. Take the time to look at the questions as you try to implement the techniques in the book. Analyze your calls using the questions and ideas contained here, and you will make progress in your ability to use them successfully. Good luck and good selling!

INDEX